GO BARLEY

go
barley

MODERN RECIPES FOR AN ANCIENT GRAIN

PAT INGLIS AND LINDA WHITWORTH
FOREWORD BY ANITA STEWART

TouchWood
Editions

TouchWood Editions
touchwoodeditions.com

LIBRARY AND ARCHIVES CANADA CATALOGUING IN PUBLICATION
Inglis, Pat, 1937–, author
    Go barley : modern recipes for an ancient grain / Pat Inglis, Linda Whitworth.

Includes index.
Issued in print and electronic formats.
ISBN 978-1-77151-051-6

    1. Cooking (Barley). I. Whitworth, Linda, 1956–, author II. Title.

TX809.B37I54 2014   641.3'316   C2013-907180-6

Editor: Cailey Cavallin
Proofreader: Christine Savage
Design: Pete Kohut
Cover and food photos by Bryce Meyer.
Landscape photos by Michael Interisano.

We gratefully acknowledge the financial support for our publishing activities
from the Government of Canada through the Canada Book Fund, Canada
Council for the Arts, and the province of British Columbia through the
British Columbia Arts Council and the Book Publishing Tax Credit.

FSC
www.fsc.org
MIX
Paper from
responsible sources
FSC® C016245

This book was produced using FSC®-certified, acid-free paper,
processed chlorine free and printed with vegetable-based inks.

1 2 3 4 5 18 17 16 15 14

PRINTED IN CANADA

To the farmers—those men and women who
make sure we have food on our tables.

CONTENTS

FOREWORD

Sometime in the year 1578, an itinerant English sailor hauled his boat ashore in what's now known as eastern Newfoundland. There he planted the first barley in North America. He wrote in his journal:

> I have in sundry places sowen Wheate, Barlie, Rie, Oates, Beanes, seeds of herbs, kernels, Plumstones, nuts, all of which prospered as in England.

Then he sailed off into the sunrise with the other fleets that landed their fishy catches on the Grand Banks.

Barley was an essential grain even then, and its story is entwined tightly with most of human settlement on this continent. It helped to set the table of North America's first feasting society, The Order of Good Cheer, in Samuel de Champlain's 1606 settlement in the Annapolis Valley at Port Royal. And in 1668, Jean Talon, the first intendent of New France, built the first Canadian brewery in Quebec City.

Since those early days, barley has been harvested all across North America. Its graceful seed heads are among the most beautiful of grains as they ripen, swaying in the summer breezes. And while the crop has generally been used in brewing and as a highly nutritious animal feed, it's role as one of the most delicious ingredients in a modern kitchen has been overlooked far too often.

Today, as we search closer to home for our food sources, and thanks to authors Pat Inglis and Linda Whitworth, barley is being recognized for its versatility, economy, and flavor.

This cookbook explores its history and nutrition while serving forth an array of wonderful recipes for every part of the menu. There's a great Black Bean Barley Salad (p. 40), a Savory Butternut Squash Barley Pilaf (p. 138), and a hearty Barley and Beef Mulligan Stew (p. 88). The Barley and Apricot Stuffed Pork Tenderloin (p. 96) could be a centrepiece for any celebration, while their Mushroom Barley Burgers (p. 123) provide inspiration for a casual vegetarian meal. At breakfast their Barley Buttermilk Pancakes (p. 16) are great served with maple syrup. And later in the day, perhaps at your coffee break, try their Chewy Caramel Squares (p. 194) or Double Chocolate Brownies (p. 197).

Go Barley is both a cookbook and a glimpse into the future of the food life of North America as we begin to collectively understand all of the reasons we need to become responsible for our own food production.

Anita Stewart
December 2013

CLOCKWISE FROM TOP LEFT: STALKS OF BARLEY, BARLEY FLAKES, PEARL BARLEY, AND HULLESS BARLEY

INTRODUCTION

The North American prairies, with their wide-open landscapes, sunny days, and cool nights, provide an ideal locale for growing barley. This ancient grain has been cultivated and eaten for thousands of years all over the world and has recently enjoyed a resurgence here at home as part of the movement to eat more local, healthy whole grain foods.

The barley industry credits much of its success to the large beef industry it feeds. Alberta's world-famous beef owes its fine white fat, gentle marbling, and unique flavor to barley. However, barley is also grown for malt and food. Malt barley grown in North America is used internationally in some of the finest beers. It is also used to flavor many products found on grocery store shelves.

As well, barley is stepping up to take its rightful place in the kitchen. It has a unique nutty flavor, a full rich texture, and a great nutrient profile. It is easy to use and comes in many forms. Pearl and pot barley have been staples in soups over the years but are now moving into the realm of risottos, salads, pilafs, and even desserts. Barley flour adds fiber and a new flavor to baked goods while maintaining their texture and taste, and barley flakes can be used as a breakfast cereal or in baking.

Newer barley products such as hulless or "naked" barley can be found on health food store shelves. This type of barley takes longer to cook but is less processed. Interestingly, barley contains fiber throughout the whole grain, so even pot and pearl barley maintain a degree of healthy fiber. Another product often available at farmers' markets or health food stores is quick-cooking barley, which, as the name suggests, makes meal preparation simple. But all barley really is easy to cook and use.

The following pages have recipes designed to please the palates of the whole family. We invite you to try these amazing dishes and join us as we "Go Barley."

HISTORY OF BARLEY

Historical texts from as far back as 8,000 BCE make reference to barley—it is one of the most ancient of the ancient grains. There is also archeological evidence that wild forms of barley were being harvested as early as 17,000 BCE.

It is believed that barley was first domesticated about 10,000 years ago in the Fertile Crescent, which includes modern-day Israel, northern Syria, Jordan, southern Turkey, and parts of Iran and Iraq. Although wild wheat from a similar time period has also been found, historians believe that barley was used far more abundantly.

Domesticated barley came from *Hordeum spontaneum*, or wild barley, which had very brittle awns that caught on the wind, allowing it to be more readily distributed. The domesticated version, *Hordeum vulgare*, was less brittle, which made collection of the grain as a food product easier. The barley we use today was likely domesticated from the original *Hordeum spontaneum* associated with ancient times.

Although barley was originally domesticated for use in food, there is evidence from as far back as 3,200 BCE that barley was also used to brew beer, which was considered part of a complete diet. As well, barley was used in ancient Egypt as treatment for a number of medical issues.

As trade routes opened, barley moved north to Europe. The Greeks used barley water for strength and health. Roman gladiators were often called "barley men" because they thought their increased strength came from eating the grain.

In the fifteenth century, barley flour was often used as the main ingredient in bread. Over the years, wheat became more popular, but today we are seeing a resurgence of interest in whole grains. This provides a wonderful opportunity to put barley back into our diets.

BARLEY NUTRITION

Barley is a great choice for health-conscious consumers who care about where their food comes from.

The media and various organizations are continually putting forward claims about the so-called benefits of "fad foods." Yet very few of these claims can actually be backed up. Health Canada and the US Federal Department of Agriculture (FDA) reviewed years of research before concluding that scientific evidence does indeed exist to support a health claim about barley products. The Canadian claim is based on evidence compiled by a team from Agriculture and Agri-Food Canada led by Dr. Nancy Ames, which indicates that the daily consumption of three grams of barley beta-glucan, a type of soluble fiber, assists in lowering cholesterol, which is a risk factor for heart disease. According to Health Canada's specifications for claims made on food labels, foods containing a minimum of one gram of beta-glucan from barley grain products can be said to meet 35 percent of the daily requirement. In the United States, the FDA now permits labels on packages of whole grain barley and foods made with barley that contain at least 0.75 grams of soluble fiber per serving to carry the following claim: "Soluble fiber from foods such as [name of food], as part of a diet low in saturated fat and cholesterol, may reduce the risk of heart disease. A serving of [name of food] supplies [x] grams of the soluble fiber necessary per day to have this effect." (For more information on the health claim, visit Health Canada at www.hc-sc.gc.ca/fn-an/label-etiquet/claims-reclam/assess-evalu/barley-orge-eng.php or the United States FDA at www.accessdata.fda.gov/scripts/cdrh/cfdocs/cfcfr/CFRSearch.cfm?fr=101.81.)

In addition, soluble fiber helps improve glycemic control, which maintains our blood sugar levels after eating. This staves off that shaky sensation sometimes felt after eating meals high in simple carbohydrates. Barley also contains insoluble fiber, which promotes digestive health. With nutritionists encouraging consumers to eat more whole grains, barley provides a new and interesting alternative to the old standbys.

Barley is a powerhouse when it comes to vitamins and minerals. It contains thiamine, niacin, folate, riboflavin, iron, calcium, potassium, phosphorus, magnesium, manganese, zinc, and selenium, all of which contribute to good overall health. The B vitamins (thiamine, niacin, folate, and riboflavin) help to make red blood cells and assist our bodies in generating energy from the food we eat. Barley also contains many of the amino acids that make up protein, which is necessary to rebuild body tissue.

Barley is low in sugar, fat, and sodium, with one half cup of cooked pearl barley (cooked in water) containing only trace amounts of sugar and fat and only 2.0 milligrams of sodium (source: Nutrient Value of Some Common Foods booklet, available from Health Canada).

Now that people want to know more about what they eat—and are trading in processed foods for whole foods that are locally grown—barley is poised to meet this demand.

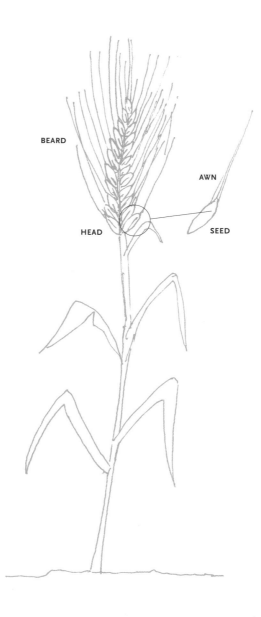

BEARD

AWN

HEAD

SEED

BARLEY BASICS

Preparing Pearl and Pot Barley

Barley is one of the original comfort foods. Its mild, slightly nutty flavor goes great with beef, bison, chicken, pork, turkey, fish, and shellfish, as well as with other grains and nuts, all kinds of vegetables, and fruit.

Barley can be cooked in a variety of liquids—beef, chicken, or vegetable broth for a savory dish, or a combination of water and fruit juice for a sweet dish or as a breakfast cereal. The length of the cooking time depends partly on how long the barley has been stored since harvest and how completely it has been processed. Barley absorbs whatever cooking liquid is used (often taking on the liquid's flavor) and expands to as much as three times its original volume. Depending on how (and how long) it's cooked, barley can be chewy nuggets in a salad, flavor-packed morsels in a stew, or a creamy base for a risotto or breakfast cereal.

The ratio of cooking liquid to barley can vary from two to one for drier cooked barley to three to one for creamier risottos and soups.

Pearl and pot barley are used interchangeably in many of the recipes in this book, although there may be slight differences in the amount of cooking liquid they require, as well as in the cooking time. If there is any excess liquid once barley is cooked, it can simply be drained.

Cooked pot and pearl barley will continue to absorb liquid, so soups, stews, and casseroles will thicken on standing or when refrigerated. When you are ready to reheat a dish, simply stir in a bit more water or broth.

Barley cooked in plain water will foam, so pay careful attention when bringing it to a boil, or add a little oil to the water before adding the barley.

The labels on packages of pearl and pot barley suggest barley be rinsed before using it in a recipe. Unless barley was purchased directly from the grower, this is not an essential step. Many cooks use it straight from the package. If you do decide to rinse before adding it to the recipe, simply place the required amount of barley in a strainer and rinse quickly under running water, then shake to drain well.

Pot and pearl barley can be cooked in several different ways.

Stovetop Simmer: Many recipes call for simmering barley in liquid in a saucepan or large skillet on the stovetop over low heat until tender, about 40 to 55 minutes. After adding the barley to the pan, bring the liquid to a boil, then reduce the heat enough to just maintain a simmer. Cover pan and begin timing the cooking. If cooked barley is sticky and you prefer separate grains, pour boiling water over the barley to rinse off surface starch, and drain well.

Oven Simmer: Pearl and pot barley may also be cooked in liquid along with other ingredients using a covered casserole dish in an oven preheated to 350°F (180°C) for 1 to 1½ hours.

Slow Cooker: The slow cooker is ideal for cooking barley when the grain is to be used as an ingredient in mouthwatering soups and stews. Generally, barley is added to other ingredients that have been pre-cooked in a skillet, such as onions, meat, poultry, and spices, just before liquid ingredients are stirred in and the mixture is poured into the slow cooker. The cooker is then covered and the food is simmered on low heat for 5 to 6 hours. If cooking on high heat, stir halfway through the cooking time to prevent the barley grains from sticking together.

Rice Cooker: Barley can also be steamed in a rice cooker. Add 1 cup (250 mL) pot or pearl barley to 2 cups (500 mL) water or chicken or vegetable broth. Vegetables such as sliced mushrooms or chopped peppers and onions that have been sautéed in a skillet may also be added. Cover rice cooker and cook for one rice cooking cycle. Fluff barley with a fork and serve as a side. Alternately, refrigerate cooked barley for future use in your favorite recipes.

Cooked barley can be stored in the refrigerator or freezer and then used as a fast addition to soups, stews, stir-fries, stuffing, casseroles, and vegetable side dishes. For each 1 cup (250 mL) of barley, use 2 cups (500 mL) of water or stock. Bring liquid to a boil. Stir in barley; reduce heat and simmer for 45 minutes. Cool. Spread on a plastic-wrap-lined baking sheet and freeze. When frozen, crumble and spoon barley into plastic freezer bags. Store cooked barley in the freezer until ready to use. Makes about 2 cups (500 mL) of cooked barley, which can be stored in the freezer for at least three months.

Cooking with Whole Barley Flour

Whole barley flour is coarser in texture than white flour, and it adds a light golden brown color and a slightly sweet nutty flavor to baked goods. Barley flour lends itself to artisan breads, cookies, and cakes made with chocolate, spice, honey, or molasses.

Whole barley flour has a shorter shelf life than white flour. Purchase in small amounts, and after dating the package, refrigerate or freeze and use within a few months. Before use, give it the sniff test. If it smells musty or has an off-odor, it has probably gone rancid and should be discarded.

Using whole barley flour instead of other flours in breads and baking will affect the final results. Start by substituting barley flour for a quarter or half of the all-purpose flour. If you're happy with the results, the next time you make the recipe increase the amount of whole barley flour and decrease the all-purpose flour.

Whole barley flour contains less gluten than wheat flour. Gluten is required to give dough elasticity and strength, so when making yeast breads and pizza crusts, it's best not to use whole barley flour for more than a quarter to a half of the total flour measurement. Also, when using barley flour, loaves of bread may have less volume.

Like pot and pearl barley, whole barley flour tends to absorb moisture when substituted for all-purpose flour in recipes, so dough and batters may appear somewhat drier. Simply add a bit more liquid.

Whole barley flour makes an excellent thickener for sauces, gravies, soups, and stews, although you may notice that mixtures are a bit less smooth than when made with white flour. Whole barley flour also makes a good coating when frying and baking.

Milling Barley Flour at Home

Though barley flour is usually available from bulk or health food stores, it can be difficult to find in regular grocery stores, depending on where you live. However, whole barley flour can be ground at home quite easily, with either a hand or electric flourmill. Purchase hulless barley and grind the amount required for your recipe. One pound (500 g) of hulless barley will make about 2¾ cups (675 mL) of flour.

RECIPES

Those of you who want to make vegetarian dishes can look for this symbol. Some of the recipes marked are already vegetarian, while the others can be easily adapted to be vegetarian-friendly (for instance, by using vegetable broth or water instead of chicken broth).

BREAKFAST

SLOW-COOKED BARLEY BREAKFAST

Imagine a breakfast that cooks while you sleep. Thick slices of apples may be added to the slow cooker along with the barley. Serve with chopped dried apricots or cranberries, fresh berries, slices of peaches, pecans, chopped dark chocolate, brown sugar or maple syrup, ground cinnamon, or milk. Leftover cooked barley can be covered and stored in the refrigerator for up to 3 days.

1 cup (250 mL) pot or pearl barley

4½ cups (1.125 L) water

2–4 Tbsp (30–60 mL) milk or water

Grease the stoneware well of a small or medium slow cooker. In it, combine barley and water. Cover and cook on low for 6 hours.

To serve, combine cooked barley with milk or water; cover and microwave on medium power for 1 to 2 minutes or until hot.

Makes 4 servings.

Nutritional Information (per serving): Calories: 176, Protein: 5 g, Carbohydrate: 39 g, Fiber: 8 g, Sugars: 0 g, Fat: 0.5 g, Saturated Fat: 0.1 g, Trans Fat: 0 g, Cholesterol: 0 mg, Sodium: 13 mg, Potassium: 143 mg

BARLEY PANCAKES WITH MAPLE YOGURT TOPPING

Whole barley flour adds fiber and nutty flavor to these pancakes. The maple yogurt topping is a delicious alternative to butter or margarine.

Pancakes

2 cups (500 mL) whole barley flour

2 Tbsp (30 mL) granulated sugar

1 Tbsp (15 mL) baking powder

¼ tsp (1 mL) salt

1 egg, beaten

3 Tbsp (45 mL) canola oil

2 cups (500 mL) milk

Topping

½ cup (125 mL) plain yogurt

2 Tbsp (30 mL) maple syrup

Fresh fruit, such as mixed berries or sliced pears, peaches, or bananas

In a medium bowl, combine barley flour, sugar, baking powder, and salt. In a smaller bowl, combine egg, oil, and milk. Stir liquid mixture into the flour mixture until just combined. Lightly grease a griddle and heat over medium-high. Pour ladlefuls of batter onto the griddle. When bubbles appear and begin to break, flip pancakes over to brown other side. Repeat with remaining batter.

In a small bowl, combine yogurt and maple syrup. To serve, place warm pancakes on serving plates and top with maple yogurt topping and fresh fruit.

Makes fourteen 4-inch (10 cm) pancakes.

Nutritional Information (per pancake, with about 1¾ tsp [9 mL] of topping): Calories: 119, Protein: 2 g, Carbohydrate: 18 g, Fiber: 2 g, Sugars: 6 g, Fat: 6 g, Saturated Fat: 0.5 g, Trans Fat: 0.1 g, Cholesterol: 16 mg, Sodium: 149 mg, Potassium: 84 mg

BARLEY BUTTERMILK PANCAKES

If you don't over-mix these pancakes, they'll be fluffy with a slight tangy flavor thanks to the reaction between the acidic buttermilk and the base baking soda. Credit the golden color and nutty flavor to the barley flour. For a variation, add ⅓ cup (75 mL) of fresh or frozen blueberries, chocolate chips, or chopped nuts to the batter.

1 cup (250 mL) whole barley flour

1 Tbsp (15 mL) granulated sugar

1 tsp (5 mL) baking powder

¼ tsp (1 mL) baking soda

¼ tsp (1 mL) salt

¾ cup (175 mL) buttermilk

1 egg

1 Tbsp (15 mL) canola oil

In a medium bowl, mix barley flour, sugar, baking powder, baking soda, and salt. In another bowl, lightly beat buttermilk, egg, and canola oil. Add liquid mixture to dry ingredients, stirring until dry ingredients are just moistened. Let stand for 5 minutes. Lightly oil a non-stick skillet and heat over medium-high. Pour ladlefuls of batter onto the skillet. Cook, flipping the pancakes to lightly brown both sides. Repeat with remaining batter. Serve immediately or keep warm until ready to serve with desired toppings.

Makes eight 4-inch (10 cm) pancakes.

Nutritional Information (per pancake): Calories: 88, Protein: 2 g, Carbohydrate: 13 g, Fiber: 2 g, Sugars: 3 g, Fat: 5 g, Saturated Fat: 0.5 g, Trans Fat: 0 g, Cholesterol: 25 mg, Sodium: 189 mg, Potassium: 40 mg

WHOLESOME GOLDEN WAFFLES

Serve these waffles for breakfast (topped with syrup, whipped cream, and fruit) or for brunch (topped with diced ham or chicken and broccoli, or diced mushrooms and other cooked vegetables, in a cream sauce [see Barley Bit]).

2¼ cups (560 mL) whole barley flour

2 Tbsp (30 mL) granulated sugar

4 tsp (20 mL) baking powder

¼ tsp (1 mL) salt

2 eggs, beaten

2¼ cups (560 mL) milk

¼ cup (60 mL) canola oil

1 tsp (5 mL) vanilla

Heat waffle iron as manufacturer directs. In a medium bowl, combine barley flour, sugar, baking powder, and salt. In a smaller bowl, combine eggs, milk, canola oil, and vanilla. Stir liquid into dry ingredients until well combined. Pour batter into the waffle iron, following manufacturer's instructions, and gently close. Remove the waffle when the lid lifts open easily, about 5 to 6 minutes. Repeat with remaining batter. Serve warm.

Makes 4 servings.

Nutritional Information (per serving): Calories: 495, Protein: 8 g, Carbohydrate: 60 g, Fiber: 8 g, Sugars: 15 g, Fat: 28 g, Saturated Fat: 2.5 g, Trans Fat: 0 g, Cholesterol: 103 mg, Sodium: 604 mg, Potassium: 238 mg

Barley Bit: To make 1 cup (250 mL) of thin cream sauce, melt 1 Tbsp (15 mL) butter or margarine in a small saucepan. Add 1 Tbsp (15 mL) whole barley flour, ⅛ tsp (0.5 mL) salt, and a dash of pepper; stir until smooth. While stirring, slowly add 1 cup (250 mL) milk. Stir and cook over medium heat until smooth and thickened, 6 to 7 minutes.

QUICK BREAKFAST BREAD

This simple-to-make quick bread is packed with the whole grain goodness of barley and wheat flours and cornmeal. Cut into squares and serve warm with eggs, bacon, sausages, or grilled tomatoes.

¾ cup (175 mL) whole barley flour

¾ cup (175 mL) whole wheat flour

½ cup (125 mL) cornmeal

2 Tbsp (30 mL) packed brown sugar

1 Tbsp (15 mL) baking powder

½ tsp (2 mL) baking soda

1 tsp (5 mL) ground cinnamon

1 tsp (5 mL) ground ginger

1 egg, beaten

1 cup (250 mL) sweetened applesauce

1 cup (250 mL) buttermilk

Preheat oven to 400°F (200°C). Grease a 9-inch (23 cm) square pan.

In a large bowl, mix barley flour, wheat flour, cornmeal, brown sugar, baking powder, baking soda, cinnamon, and ginger. In another bowl, combine egg, applesauce, and buttermilk. Stir mixture into dry ingredients, mixing well. Pour batter into prepared pan. Bake in the oven for 25 to 30 minutes or until a cake tester or toothpick inserted in the center of the bread comes out clean.

Makes 8 servings.

Nutritional Information (per serving): Calories: 160, Protein: 4 g, Carbohydrate: 33 g, Fiber: 4 g, Sugars: 10 g, Fat: 3 g, Saturated Fat: 0.5 g, Trans Fat: 0 g, Cholesterol: 25 mg, Sodium: 258 mg, Potassium: 146 mg

BASIC WHOLE BARLEY CRÊPES

If crêpes are made in advance, stack them between parchment paper, wrap, and refrigerate for 1 day or freeze for as long as 1 month. For a savory brunch or lunch, fill the crêpes with diced chicken or ham or cooked vegetables in a thin cream sauce (see Barley Bit on p. 19). For sweeter dessert crêpes, add 2 teaspoons (10 mL) of granulated sugar to the flour. Fill with poached apples or peaches and top with a puff of whipped cream.

½ cup (125 mL) whole barley flour

Pinch salt

1 egg, lightly beaten

⅔ cup (150 mL) milk

½ tsp (2 mL) canola oil, for brushing

In a bowl, combine flour and salt; add egg. Whisk in milk until mixture is smooth. Heat a small non-stick skillet or crêpe pan (6 to 8 inches [15–20 cm]) over medium-high. Brush bottom of pan with oil. Add 2 tablespoons (30 mL) of batter and quickly tilt pan to cover bottom with batter. Shake pan to loosen crêpe and cook until edges of crêpe begin to curl and it no longer sticks to the pan, about 30 seconds. Gently flip crêpe over and cook for a few seconds. Remove from pan and set aside. Repeat with remaining batter.

Makes about 8 crêpes.

Nutritional Information (per crêpe): Calories: 44, Protein: 1 g, Carbohydrate: 6 g, Fiber: 2 g, Sugars: 1 g, Fat: 2 g, Saturated Fat: 0.4 g, Trans Fat: 0 g, Cholesterol: 25 mg, Sodium: 26 mg, Potassium: 38 mg

CHICKEN AND MUSHROOM CRÊPES

These chicken and mushroom filled crêpes are a tempting late breakfast or brunch treat. To make things easier in the morning, prepare the crêpes the night before. If you like, you can sprinkle the cooked crêpes with shredded cheddar cheese just before serving.

⅓ cup (75 mL) butter or margarine

½ cup (125 mL) sliced mushrooms

¼ cup (60 mL) whole barley flour

2 cups (500 mL) milk

¼ tsp (1 mL) salt

¼ tsp (1 mL) pepper

1¾ cups (425 mL) diced cooked chicken

8 Basic Whole Barley Crêpes (p. 21)

Preheat oven to 400°F (200°C). Grease an 8-inch (20 cm) square baking dish.

In a medium saucepan over medium-high, heat butter or margarine. Add mushrooms and lightly brown. Add flour, stirring until completely mixed in. Gradually stir in milk; cook until thickened, stirring constantly. Stir in salt and pepper. Remove pan from heat. Set aside ¾ cup (175 mL) of the sauce and stir chicken into remaining sauce.

Spoon about ¼ cup (60 mL) of the chicken mixture onto each crêpe and gently fold each side of the crêpe to the middle. Place the crêpes seam-side down in the baking dish. Top with reserved sauce and bake for 10 to 15 minutes or until hot.

Makes 4 servings (8 crêpes).

Nutritional Information (per crêpe): Calories: 211, Protein: 15 g, Carbohydrate: 12 g, Fiber: 1 g, Sugars: 4 g, Fat: 13 g, Saturated Fat: 6 g, Trans Fat: 0.3 g, Cholesterol: 77 mg, Sodium: 212 mg, Potassium: 147 mg

BARLEY GRANOLA OF GRAINS, NUTS, AND FRUIT

Barley flakes are combined with oats, coconut, and a variety of nuts and seeds and then toasted to a golden brown to make this wholesome breakfast cereal or nutritious snack. Granola should be stored in an airtight container.

2 cups (500 mL) barley flakes

2 cups (500 mL) quick-cooking rolled oats

½ cup (125 mL) unsweetened shredded coconut

½ cup (125 mL) walnut pieces

½ cup (125 mL) pecan pieces

¼ cup (60 mL) raw sunflower seeds

¼ cup (60 mL) raw sesame seeds

1 tsp (5 mL) ground cinnamon

⅔ cup (150 mL) liquid honey

1 tsp (5 mL) vanilla

1½ cups (375 mL) raisins or dried cranberries

Preheat the oven to 300°F (150°C). Lightly grease 2 baking sheets.

In a large bowl, combine barley flakes, rolled oats, coconut, walnuts, pecans, sunflower seeds, sesame seeds, and cinnamon. In a small bowl, combine honey and vanilla. Pour over dry mixture and toss thoroughly. Spread granola on prepared baking sheets and bake for 20 minutes or until golden brown, stirring halfway through so mixture browns evenly. Remove trays from oven. Stir in raisins or cranberries and let granola cool completely. Once granola is cooled, remove from sheets and store in an airtight container.

Makes 8 servings (1 cup [250 mL] each).

Nutritional Information (per serving): Calories: 524, Protein: 11 g, Carbohydrate: 83 g, Fiber: 9 g, Sugars: 45 g, Fat: 19 g, Saturated Fat: 4.5 g, Trans Fat: 0 g, Cholesterol: 0 mg, Sodium: 16 mg, Potassium: 312 mg

GRANOLA AND FRUIT YOGURT PARFAIT Ⓥ

For a special breakfast or lunch buffet, prepare this recipe in one large (approximately 10-cup [2.5 L]) glass serving bowl using 3 cups (750 mL) of seasonal fresh fruit.

4 cups (1 L) Barley Granola (p. 24), divided into 16 equal parts

1½ cups (375 mL) vanilla 2% yogurt, divided into 12 equal parts

1 banana, thinly sliced

8 strawberries, sliced

Spoon 1 part barley granola into each of 4 parfait or deep dessert dishes. Top each with a layer of yogurt. Add another layer of granola to each dish, then one-quarter of the banana slices. Spoon another layer of yogurt and then a layer of barley granola into each dish. Top each with 1 sliced strawberry, a spoonful of yogurt, and a sprinkle of granola. Spoon remaining sliced strawberries overtop of each parfait.

Makes 4 servings.

Nutritional Information (per serving): Calories: 618, Protein: 18 g, Carbohydrate: 96 g, Fiber: 11 g, Sugars: 53 g, Fat: 21 g, Saturated Fat: 6 g, Trans Fat: 0 g, Cholesterol: 6 mg, Sodium: 45 mg, Potassium: 473 mg

BRUNCH HASH BAKED EGGS

Cooked barley, eggs, and sausage combine perfectly to form this hearty and delicious breakfast or brunch dish that can be prepared ahead of time. Add the egg at the last minute, just before popping everything into the oven. If using barley you've cooked ahead of time and stored in the fridge, add 3 to 4 extra minutes to the cooking time.

1 can (10 oz [284 mL]) condensed less-sodium chicken broth, undiluted

1⅓ cups (325 mL) water

1 cup (250 mL) pot or pearl barley

1½ tsp (7 mL) canola oil

8 oz (250 g) breakfast sausage, diced

½ cup (125 mL) chopped onion

1 garlic clove, minced

¼ cup (60 mL) chopped parsley

4 eggs

Pinch salt and pepper

In a medium saucepan over high heat, bring chicken broth and water to a boil. Add barley; return to a boil. Reduce heat; cover pan and simmer for 45 to 50 minutes, until barley is tender. Strain if necessary.

Preheat oven to 375°F (190°C). Lightly grease 4 ramekins or oven-safe single serving dishes.

In a large skillet over medium-high, heat oil; add sausage, onion, and garlic, and cook until sausage is brown. Drain off excess fat and add cooked barley. Stir and cook until barley just begins to brown. Stir in parsley. Remove pan from heat.

Spoon approximately 1 cup (250 mL) sausage barley hash into each ramekin. Break an egg into each dish and sprinkle with salt and pepper. Place ramekins in the oven, directly on the rack. Bake for 10 to 15 minutes or until yolk is set and white is no longer runny.

Makes 4 servings.

Nutritional Information (per serving): Calories: 492, Protein: 26 g, Carbohydrate: 45 g, Fiber: 8 g, Sugars: 1 g, Fat: 24 g, Saturated Fat: 8 g, Trans Fat: 0 g, Cholesterol: 233 mg, Sodium: 809 mg, Potassium: 316 mg

BREAKFAST COOKIES

Wholesome cookies or little sweet cakes can occasionally stand in for a full breakfast when you're pinched for time, especially when accompanied by a glass of milk or a bowl of yogurt. These cookies are made with the nutritious ingredients of barley flour, barley flakes, oats, and a mixture of dried fruit, seeds, and nuts. They are also great with mid-morning coffee or as an after-school snack.

¾ cup (175 mL) whole barley flour

½ cup (125 mL) all-purpose flour

½ tsp (2 mL) baking powder

½ tsp (2 mL) baking soda

½ tsp (2 mL) ground cinnamon

½ cup (125 mL) butter or margarine, softened

¾ cup (175 mL) packed brown sugar

2 eggs

¼ cup (60 mL) sweetened applesauce

1 cup (250 mL) barley flakes

1 cup (250 mL) quick-cooking rolled oats

3 Tbsp (45 mL) whole flaxseed

½ cup (125 mL) raisins

¼ cup (60 mL) raw sunflower seeds

¼ cup (60 mL) slivered almonds

Preheat oven to 350°F (180°C). Lightly grease a baking sheet.

In a medium bowl, combine barley flour, all-purpose flour, baking powder, baking soda, and cinnamon. In a large bowl, cream butter or margarine; beat in brown sugar, then eggs and applesauce. Stir in flour mixture, then barley flakes, rolled oats, flaxseed, raisins, sunflower seeds, and almonds.

Drop ¼ cup (60 mL) scoops of dough onto prepared baking sheet, 2½ inches (6 cm) apart. Bake for 17 to 18 minutes or until golden brown.

Makes 18 cookies.

Nutritional Information (per cookie): Calories: 198, Protein: 4 g, Carbohydrate: 28 g, Fiber: 3 g, Sugars: 13 g, Fat: 8 g, Saturated Fat: 3.5 g, Trans Fat: 0.2 g, Cholesterol: 35 mg, Sodium: 104 mg, Potassium: 86 mg

APPETIZERS, SALADS, AND SOUPS

PRAIRIE CRANBERRY ALMOND CRISPS

These crisp breads are delicious topped or spread with a soft cheese like Boursin, brie, or chèvre.

1½ cups (375 mL) all-purpose flour

¾ cup (175 mL) whole barley flour

1 Tbsp (15 mL) packed brown sugar

1½ tsp (7 mL) baking soda

¼ tsp (1 mL) salt

2 Tbsp (30 mL) canola oil

2 Tbsp (30 mL) honey

1½ cups (375 mL) buttermilk

1 cup (250 mL) blanched sliced almonds

½ cup (125 mL) dried cranberries

¼ cup (60 mL) raw sunflower seeds

3 Tbsp (45 mL) whole flaxseed

Preheat oven to 375°F (190°C). Grease a 9 × 5 inch (23 × 13 cm) loaf pan, or line pan with parchment paper.

In a large bowl, combine all-purpose flour, barley flour, brown sugar, baking soda, and salt. Stir in oil and honey, then buttermilk. Add almonds, cranberries, sunflower seeds, and flaxseed. Spoon batter into loaf pan and bake on middle rack until a cake tester or toothpick inserted in the center of the loaf comes out clean, approximately 45 minutes. Let cool in pan on a cooling rack for 5 minutes, then turn out onto rack and let cool completely.

Wrap loaf in plastic food wrap and freeze until easy to slice, about 2 hours.

After removing loaf from freezer, preheat oven to 300°F (150°C). Grease or line a baking sheet with parchment paper and set aside until needed.

With a serrated knife, cut the loaf into ¼-inch (6 mm) thick slices, then cut slices in half crosswise. Place on prepared baking sheet and bake until browned and crisp, about 30 minutes, rotating the baking sheet and turning the crisps over halfway through. Remove from oven and cool on sheets on a cooling rack.

Makes 36 crisps.

Nutritional Information (per crisp): Calories: 74, Protein: 2 g, Carbohydrate: 10 g, Fiber: 1 g, Sugars: 3 g, Fat: 3 g, Saturated Fat: 0.3 g, Trans Fat: 0 g, Cholesterol: 0 mg, Sodium: 80 mg, Potassium: 48 mg

BARLEY HERB LOAF

Spread thin slices of this herb-flavored loaf with Boursin or goat cheese. Or spread with pâté and top with a small piece of sweet-and-sour pickle.

2 cups (500 mL) whole barley flour

1 cup (250 mL) all-purpose flour

1 tsp (5 mL) baking powder

½ tsp (2 mL) baking soda

1 Tbsp (15 mL) chopped fresh parsley

1 tsp (5 mL) dried dill weed

½ tsp (2 mL) dried oregano

½ tsp (2 mL) dried basil

½ tsp (2 mL) dried thyme

½ tsp (2 mL) dried marjoram

½ tsp (2 mL) salt

¼ cup (60 mL) canola oil

¼ cup (60 mL) honey

2 eggs

1 cup (250 mL) plain yogurt

1 tsp (5 mL) raw sesame seeds

Preheat oven to 350°F (180°C). Lightly grease a 9 × 5 inch (23 × 13 cm) loaf pan.

In a large bowl, combine barley flour, all-purpose flour, baking powder, baking soda, parsley, dill, oregano, basil, thyme, marjoram, and salt. In a medium bowl, mix oil and honey. Add eggs and beat well; stir in yogurt. Stir the liquid ingredients into the flour mixture until just moistened. Spoon batter into loaf pan. Sprinkle sesame seeds on top. Bake in the oven for 40 minutes or until a toothpick inserted into the center of the loaf comes out clean. Let cool in the pan for 10 minutes. Remove from the pan and let cool on a cooling rack. Store in an airtight container.

Makes 1 loaf (approximately 18 slices).

Nutritional Information (per slice): Calories: 125, Protein: 2 g, Carbohydrate: 19 g, Fiber: 2 g, Sugars: 5 g, Fat: 6 g, Saturated Fat: 0.5 g, Trans Fat: 0 g, Cholesterol: 22 mg, Sodium: 139 mg, Potassium: 54 mg

SUNFLOWER BARLEY CRACKERS

Use your coffee grinder, blender, or food processor to grind the sunflower seeds needed for these crisp crackers. The crackers are delicious sprinkled with sunflower seeds and served with pâté, cheese, and fruit.

1 cup (250 mL) whole barley flour

¼ tsp (1 mL) salt

½ cup (125 mL) finely ground sunflower seeds

3 Tbsp (45 mL) canola oil

3 Tbsp (45 mL) water

Preheat oven to 350°F (180°C).

Combine barley flour, salt, ground sunflower seeds, and canola oil. Gradually add just enough water to form a soft dough. Knead dough and roll out on a lightly floured surface to ⅛-inch (3 mm) thickness. Cut into shapes and prick each cracker several times with a fork. Arrange on a baking sheet. Bake for 10 minutes or until lightly browned.

Makes about 30 crackers.

Nutritional Information (per cracker): Calories: 36, Protein: 0 g, Carbohydrate: 3 g, Fiber: 1 g, Sugars: 0 g, Fat: 3 g, Saturated Fat: 0.2 g, Trans Fat: 0 g, Cholesterol: 0 mg, Sodium: 20 mg, Potassium: 14 mg

GRAIN AND SPINACH STUFFED PORTOBELLO MUSHROOMS

These baked mushroom caps are piled with a savory barley spinach stuffing and sprinkled with cheese. They make an eye-catching appetizer or a vegetarian main dish when served with a salad and crusty rolls.

4 large portobello mushrooms

2 tsp (10 mL) canola oil

¼ cup (60 mL) chopped onion

1 garlic clove, minced

½ cup (125 mL) pot or pearl barley

2 cups (500 mL) less-sodium vegetable or chicken broth

¼ cup (60 mL) whole grain bulgar

½ tsp (2 mL) dried summer savory

¼ tsp (1 mL) salt

¼ tsp (1 mL) pepper

8 cups (2 L) fresh spinach leaves, thinly sliced crosswise

¼ cup (60 mL) shredded Swiss, Monterey Jack, or Parmesan cheese

Remove stems from mushrooms; coarsely chop stems. In a medium saucepan over medium-high, heat oil and sauté onion, garlic, and mushroom stems for 1 minute. Stir in barley. Add broth, then bring to a boil. Reduce heat, cover pan, and simmer for 30 minutes. Stir in bulgar and continue to simmer for 12 to 15 minutes or until grains are almost tender. Stir in savory, salt, and pepper. Stir in spinach. Cover pan and simmer for 4 minutes or until spinach is wilted.

Preheat oven to 375°F (190°C). Line an ovenproof pan with aluminum foil.

Use a spoon or sharp knife to scrape gills from mushroom caps; discard gills. Place caps, rounded side down, in prepared pan. Once spinach mixture is cooked, spoon it into the mushroom caps and sprinkle with cheese. Bake for 18 to 20 minutes or until mushrooms are tender and cheese is slightly melted.

Makes 4 servings.

Nutritional Information (per serving): Calories: 228, Protein: 11 g, Carbohydrate: 37 g, Fiber: 9 g, Sugars: 3 g, Fat: 5 g, Saturated Fat: 1.5 g, Trans Fat: 0 g, Cholesterol: 6 mg, Sodium: 342 mg, Potassium: 438 mg

BLACK BEAN BARLEY SALAD

The combination of barley, black beans, and cheese provides enough protein to make this a vegetarian main dish salad. Or, if desired, top the salad with warm slices of grilled chicken breast or a skewer of grilled shrimp. The barley bean mixture can be put together the day before, making meal preparation a snap.

2 tsp (10 mL) canola oil

½ cup (125 mL) pot or pearl barley

2 cups (500 mL) less-sodium vegetable broth or water

1 can (19 oz [540 mL]) black beans, drained and rinsed

1 small yellow bell pepper, thinly sliced

8 cherry tomatoes, halved

½ cup (125 mL) corn kernels

¼ cup (60 mL) chopped chives

3 Tbsp (45 mL) lime juice

¼ cup (60 mL) olive oil

½ tsp (2 mL) salt

¼ tsp (1 mL) pepper

6 large lettuce leaves

¼ cup (60 mL) shredded cheddar or Monterey Jack cheese

In a medium saucepan over medium-high, heat oil. Add barley and sauté for 3 minutes. Add vegetable broth or water and bring to a boil. Reduce heat to simmer. Cover and cook for 30 minutes; drain and cool.

In a large bowl, combine cooked barley, black beans, yellow pepper, tomatoes, corn, and chives. In a small bowl, combine lime juice, olive oil, salt, and pepper; pour over barley mixture and toss. Serve over lettuce and top with shredded cheese.

Makes 6 servings.

Nutritional Information (per serving): Calories: 271, Protein: 8 g, Carbohydrate: 32 g, Fiber: 8 g, Sugars: 3 g, Fat: 13 g, Saturated Fat: 2.5 g, Trans Fat: 0 g, Cholesterol: 5 mg, Sodium: 560 mg, Potassium: 170 mg

WILD RICE, BARLEY, AND FRUIT SALAD

Here's the perfect salad to bring to a potluck supper. It can be made ahead, and it's easy to transport.

1 cup (250 mL) pecans
1 cup (250 mL) pot or pearl barley
¼ cup (60 mL) wild rice
4½ cups (1.125 L) water
¾ cup (175 mL) brown rice
1 orange
2 green onions, chopped
¾ cup (175 mL) dried apricots, chopped
¾ cup (175 mL) dried cranberries
½ cup (125 mL) orange juice
1 garlic clove, minced
3 Tbsp (45 mL) balsamic vinegar
2 tsp (10 mL) Dijon mustard
¼ cup (60 mL) olive oil
¼ tsp (1 mL) salt
¼ tsp (1 mL) pepper
½ cup (125 mL) chopped parsley

Preheat oven to 350°F (180°C).

On an ungreased baking pan, spread pecans evenly. Bake for 5 minutes, then coarsely chop and set aside. Rinse barley and wild rice under cold running water; drain. In a medium saucepan over high heat, bring measured water to a boil and stir in wild rice and barley. Reduce heat to simmer. Cover pan and cook for 35 minutes. Add brown rice, then cover pan and simmer for another 25 minutes. Cool.

Peel and seed the orange and cut it into small pieces. In a large bowl, mix orange pieces, green onions, apricots, and cranberries with barley rice mixture.

In a small bowl, combine orange juice, garlic, vinegar, and mustard. Whisk in oil as well as salt and pepper to taste. Toss dressing with barley mixture; sprinkle with toasted pecans and parsley.

Makes 10 servings.

Nutritional Information (per serving): Calories: 326, Protein: 5 g, Carbohydrate: 49 g, Fiber: 6 g, Sugars: 14 g, Fat: 14 g, Saturated Fat: 1.5 g, Trans Fat: 0 g, Cholesterol: 0 mg, Sodium: 99 mg, Potassium: 346 mg

(V) # ASIAN BARLEY AND WILD RICE SALAD

One of Linda's favorites, this salad combines wild rice with barley, red peppers, green onions, and corn, and is then dressed with the Asian flavors of soy sauce, rice vinegar, and sesame oil. Toasted pecans add crunch.

2 cups (500 mL) chopped pecans

1 cup (250 mL) wild rice

4 cups (1 L) chicken or vegetable broth, or water

1 cup (250 mL) pot or pearl barley

2 medium sweet red peppers, chopped

¼ cup (60 mL) chopped green onions

2 cups (500 mL) frozen corn kernels, thawed

⅓ cup (75 mL) soy sauce

⅓ cup (75 mL) rice vinegar

¼ cup (60 mL) sesame oil

Preheat oven to 350°F (180°C). On an ungreased baking pan, spread pecan pieces evenly. Bake for 5 minutes. Remove from oven and let cool.

In a large saucepan over high heat, bring wild rice and broth or water to a boil. Reduce heat and simmer for 15 to 20 minutes. Add barley and continue simmering for an additional 40 minutes. Cover pan and let stand until all moisture is absorbed. Cool.

Put barley mixture in a large serving bowl. Add peppers, onions, corn, soy sauce, rice vinegar, and sesame oil; mix well. Place in fridge for 2 hours or overnight. Add pecans just before serving.

Makes approximately 12 servings.

Nutritional Information (per serving): Calories: 312, Protein: 7 g, Carbohydrate: 32 g, Fiber: 6 g, Sugars: 4 g, Fat: 18 g, Saturated Fat: 2 g, Trans Fat: 0 g, Cholesterol: 0 mg, Sodium: 719 mg, Potassium: 291 mg

MEXICAN BARLEY SALAD

This is one salad that actually improves when made ahead and refrigerated, providing time for the Mexican flavors of chili and cumin to blend with cooked barley, corn, tomatoes, and green pepper. To make a vegetarian version, substitute vegetable broth for the chicken broth.

1 cup (250 mL) pot or pearl barley

1 can (10 oz [284 mL]) condensed less-sodium chicken broth, undiluted

1¼ cups (310 mL) water

⅓ cup (75 mL) canola oil

⅓ cup (75 mL) cider vinegar

1 garlic clove, minced

½ tsp (2 mL) chili powder

½ tsp (2 mL) ground cumin

1 can (12 oz [341 mL]) corn kernels, drained

2 tomatoes, coarsely chopped

1 small green pepper, coarsely chopped

4 green onions, sliced

¼ cup (60 mL) minced fresh parsley or cilantro

In a medium saucepan over high heat, combine barley, chicken broth, and water. Bring to a boil. Reduce heat to simmer; cover pan and cook for 40 minutes. Allow barley to cool and then place it in a large bowl.

In a small bowl, combine canola oil, cider vinegar, garlic, chili powder, and cumin. Pour over barley and toss well. Stir in corn, tomatoes, green pepper, and green onions. Garnish with minced parsley or cilantro. Refrigerate until ready to serve.

Makes 8 servings.

Nutritional Information (per serving): Calories: 204, Protein: 4 g, Carbohydrate: 27 g, Fiber: 5 g, Sugars: 3 g, Fat: 10 g, Saturated Fat: 1 g, Trans Fat: 0 g, Cholesterol: 0 mg, Sodium: 73 mg, Potassium: 294 mg

ZUCCHINI, BEAN, AND ALMOND SALAD

In this refreshing summer salad, cooked barley is tossed with kidney beans, red pepper, zucchini, and green onions, then garnished with toasted slivered almonds. This salad is particularly good with barbecued flank steak, sautéed fish, or served as a vegetarian main course.

½ cup (125 mL) slivered almonds

2 cups (500 mL) vegetable broth

1 cup (250 mL) pot or pearl barley

1 can (14 oz [398 mL]) kidney beans, drained and rinsed

1 large sweet red pepper, diced

¾ cup (175 mL) diced zucchini

⅓ cup (75 mL) diced green onions

2 Tbsp (30 mL) olive oil

1 Tbsp (15 mL) balsamic vinegar

¼ tsp (1 mL) salt

¼ tsp (1 mL) pepper

Preheat oven to 350°F (180°C). On an ungreased baking pan, spread almonds evenly. Bake for 10 minutes or until golden brown, stirring once or twice to ensure even browning.

In a medium saucepan over high heat, bring vegetable broth to a boil and stir in barley. Reduce heat to simmer, cover pan, and cook for 30 minutes. Drain and allow to cool.

In a large salad bowl, place kidney beans, red pepper, zucchini, green onions, and cooled barley. In a small bowl, blend oil, vinegar, salt, and pepper. Drizzle over salad and toss well. Garnish with toasted almonds.

Makes 8 servings.

Nutritional Information (per serving): Calories: 212, Protein: 7 g, Carbohydrate: 31 g, Fiber: 8 g, Sugars: 3 g, Fat: 7 g, Saturated Fat: 1 g, Trans Fat: 0 g, Cholesterol: 0 mg, Sodium: 440 mg, Potassium: 206 mg

BARLEY TABBOULEH

Garnish this Middle Eastern dish with mint leaves and serve it icy cold as a salad or as an appetizer with crisp bread. Add the tomatoes just before serving to keep their firm texture and taste.

1 cup (250 mL) pot or pearl barley

2 cups (500 mL) water

1 cup (250 mL) chopped fresh parsley

½ cup (125 mL) chopped fresh mint

½ cup (125 mL) chopped green or red onion

1 small cucumber, coarsely chopped

¼ cup (60 mL) olive oil

¼ cup (60 mL) fresh lemon juice

½ tsp (2 mL) ground cinnamon

¾ tsp (4 mL) salt

Freshly ground black pepper, to taste

3 plum tomatoes, chopped

Fresh mint leaves, for garnish

In a saucepan over high heat, combine barley and water; bring to a boil. Reduce heat to simmer; cover pan and cook for 40 minutes, then chill. In a large bowl, combine chilled barley, parsley, and mint. Add onion and cucumber. In a small bowl, whisk together olive oil, lemon juice, cinnamon, salt, and pepper; pour over barley mixture and mix well, then refrigerate. Shortly before serving, stir in tomatoes. Garnish with fresh mint leaves.

Makes 8 servings.

Nutritional Information (per serving): Calories: 161, Protein: 3 g, Carbohydrate: 22 g, Fiber: 5 g, Sugars: 1 g, Fat: 7 g, Saturated Fat: 1 g, Trans Fat: 0 g, Cholesterol: 0 mg, Sodium: 231 mg, Potassium: 209 mg

LAYERED BARLEY, HAM, AND TOMATO SALAD

This salad looks spectacular layered in a tall glass bowl. If using in a buffet, set the bowl on a container of crushed ice.

1 Tbsp (15 mL) canola oil

3 Tbsp (45 mL) chopped onion

⅓ cup (75 mL) pot or pearl barley

1 cup (250 mL) less-sodium chicken broth

4 cups (1 L) torn mixed salad greens

⅓ cup (75 mL) thinly sliced red onion

1½ cups (375 mL) diced cooked ham

1½ cups (375 mL) halved grape tomatoes

½ cup (125 mL) pitted and sliced kalamata olives

¾ cup (175 mL) diced English cucumber

½ cup (125 mL) balsamic or sun-dried tomato salad dressing

In a medium saucepan over medium-high, heat oil. Add onion and sauté until softened, about 2 minutes. Stir in barley and chicken broth. Bring to a boil; cover pan and reduce heat to simmer for 40 minutes, then cool.

In a large, tall glass serving bowl, layer salad greens and red onion. Spoon cooked barley overtop, then layer ham, tomatoes, olives, and cucumber. Store in the refrigerator until ready to serve. Add dressing just before serving and toss lightly.

Makes 6 servings.

Nutritional Information (per serving): Calories: 191, Protein: 8 g, Carbohydrate: 17 g, Fiber: 3 g, Sugars: 5 g, Fat: 11 g, Saturated Fat: 1.5 g, Trans Fat: 0 g, Cholesterol: 16 mg, Sodium: 628 mg, Potassium: 136 mg

COUNTRY MUSHROOM BARLEY SOUP

For extra flavor, stir in ½ cup (125 mL) of dry sherry along with cooked barley.

½ cup (125 mL) pot or pearl barley

1 carton (32 oz [900 mL]) less-sodium, ready-to-use chicken broth, divided

2½ cups (625 mL) boiling water

1 oz (30 g) dried porcini mushrooms

2 Tbsp (30 mL) canola oil

4 medium shallots, minced

8 cups (2 L) sliced white or brown mushrooms

3 celery stalks, finely chopped

1 tsp (5 mL) dried sage

¼ tsp (1 mL) salt

¼ tsp (1 mL) pepper

2 Tbsp (30 mL) whole barley flour

½ cup (125 mL) reduced fat sour cream (optional)

4 tsp (20 mL) chopped chives

In a medium saucepan over high heat, bring barley and 1½ cups (375 mL) of the broth to a boil; cover pan and reduce heat. Simmer barley until tender, about 40 minutes.

Meanwhile, in a medium bowl, pour boiling water over porcini mushrooms and soak for about 20 minutes until softened. Pour mushrooms and soaking liquid through a sieve set over a container to reserve the soaking liquid, pressing gently to squeeze the liquid out of the mushrooms. Finely chop the mushrooms.

In a Dutch oven or large saucepan over medium, heat oil. Add shallots and cook until softened, about 2 minutes. Add sliced mushrooms; stir and cook for 8 to 10 minutes, until they start to brown. Stir in porcini mushrooms, celery, sage, salt, and pepper, and cook for about 3 minutes. Sprinkle mixture with barley flour; cook and stir until flour is mixed in. Add soaking liquid and remaining broth. Bring to a boil, then reduce heat and simmer, stirring occasionally until soup has thickened, about 20 minutes. Add cooked barley and simmer until heated through, about 4 minutes. If desired, just before serving, spoon a quarter of the sour cream into the center of each portion. Garnish each serving with chives.

Makes 4 servings (1¾ cups [425 mL] each).

Nutritional Information (per serving, without sour cream): Calories: 275, Protein: 14 g, Carbohydrate: 38 g, Fiber: 8 g, Sugars: 6 g, Fat: 8 g, Saturated Fat: 1 g, Trans Fat: 0 g, Cholesterol: 5 mg, Sodium: 319 mg, Potassium: 601 mg

COLORFUL BEAN, VEGETABLE, AND BARLEY SOUP

This vegetarian soup is packed with nutrients provided by barley, kidney beans, tomatoes, and fresh kale. A base of ready-to-use, organic vegetable broth keeps the salt content low.

1 Tbsp (15 mL) canola oil

1 medium onion, chopped

3 carrots, sliced

2 celery stalks, sliced

⅓ cup (75 mL) pot or pearl barley

1 carton (32 oz [900 mL]) ready-to-use, organic vegetable broth

1 cup (250 mL) water

1 can (19 oz [540 mL]) red kidney beans, drained and rinsed

3 large plum tomatoes, diced

2 cups (500 mL) firmly packed chopped fresh kale leaves, stems and ribs removed

¼ tsp (1 mL) pepper

In a large saucepan over medium-high, heat oil. Add onion, carrots, and celery, then cook until tender, about 5 minutes. Stir in barley, broth, water, beans, and tomatoes. Heat to a boil. Cover pan, reduce heat, and cook for 50 minutes or until barley is tender. Stir in kale. Cover pan and continue cooking until kale is wilted, about 3 to 4 minutes. Add pepper and serve hot.

Makes 6 servings (1¼ cups [310 mL] each).

Nutritional Information (per serving): Calories: 189, Protein: 9 g, Carbohydrate: 34 g, Fiber: 9 g, Sugars: 6 g, Fat: 3 g, Saturated Fat: 0.3 g, Trans Fat: 0 g, Cholesterol: 0 mg, Sodium: 453 mg, Potassium: 317 mg

LENTIL, BARLEY, AND YAM SOUP

For Pat, a supply of homemade barley soups is like gold in the freezer. On a busy fall or winter night, supper can be a bowl of hot soup, a salad, and bread. This soup combines nutritious barley and green lentils with yam, carrots, and celery. It's equally good when made with chicken or vegetable broth. The cooked soup can be covered and refrigerated for up to 2 days or kept longer in the freezer. Just add more broth when reheating.

½ cup (125 mL) green lentils

2 tsp (10 mL) canola oil

2 garlic cloves, minced

2 carrots, coarsely chopped

3 celery stalks, chopped

1 medium onion, chopped

1½ tsp (7 mL) dried thyme

½ cup (125 mL) pot or pearl barley

6 cups (1.5 L) less-sodium chicken or vegetable broth

2 bay leaves

1 medium yam, peeled and diced

¼ cup (60 mL) fresh dill, chopped (or 1¼ tsp [6 mL] dried dill)

¼ cup (60 mL) fresh parsley, chopped

¼ tsp (1 mL) salt

¼ tsp (1 mL) pepper

Rinse lentils, discarding any blemished or shriveled ones; set aside. In a large saucepan over medium, heat oil. Sauté garlic, carrots, celery, onion, and thyme, stirring often, for about 5 minutes or until vegetables are softened.

Stir in lentils and barley; pour in broth. Add bay leaves. Bring to a boil. Reduce heat, cover pan, and simmer for 40 minutes. Stir in yam; cover pan and simmer for 20 minutes or until barley and yam are tender. Remove and discard bay leaves. Stir in dill and parsley. Season with salt and pepper. Add more broth if the soup is too thick.

Makes 8 servings (1¼ cups [310 mL] each).

Nutritional Information (per serving): Calories: 141, Protein: 8 g, Carbohydrate: 24 g, Fiber: 5 g, Sugars: 4 g, Fat: 2 g, Saturated Fat: 0.5 g, Trans Fat: 0 g, Cholesterol: 4 mg, Sodium: 215 mg

CREAMY TOMATO BARLEY SOUP

Crushed tomatoes, barley, and light cream are combined to produce this hearty, creamy tomato soup. Made with less-sodium vegetable broth, it makes a tasty vegetarian lunch or supper when served with a side salad and rolls.

2 Tbsp (30 mL) canola oil

1 small onion, chopped

1 garlic clove, minced

⅔ cup (150 mL) pot or pearl barley

2 cans (28 oz [796 mL] each) crushed tomatoes

1 carton (32 oz [900 mL]) less-sodium, ready-to-use vegetable or chicken broth

1 cup (250 mL) water

1 Tbsp (15 mL) fresh basil, chopped (or 1 tsp [5 mL] dried basil)

¼ tsp (1 mL) salt

¼ tsp (1 mL) pepper

1 cup (250 mL) light cream

In a large saucepan or Dutch oven over medium-high, heat oil. Add onion and garlic and cook for 5 minutes, stirring occasionally. Stir in barley, tomatoes, broth, and water. Bring to a boil, then reduce heat. Cover pan and simmer for 50 minutes, stirring occasionally, until barley is tender. Stir in basil, salt, pepper, and cream.

Makes 8 servings (1¼ cups [310 mL] each).

Nutritional Information (per serving): Calories: 227, Protein: 6 g, Carbohydrate: 32 g, Fiber: 7 g, Sugars: 2 g, Fat: 10 g, Saturated Fat: 4 g, Trans Fat: 0.2 g, Cholesterol: 20 mg, Sodium: 438 mg, Potassium: 730 mg

MISO VEGETABLE SOUP

V

Miso is a Japanese fermented soybean product. It is available in different flavors, with the light yellow being the mildest and the golden variety deeper in flavor. Long, slow cooking develops the rich flavors of the barley and the vegetables.

1 Tbsp (15 mL) canola oil

4 carrots, peeled and diced

4 celery stalks, diced

1 small onion, finely chopped

1 tsp (5 mL) dried thyme

¼ tsp (1 mL) coarsely ground black pepper

1 cup (250 mL) pot or pearl barley

2 cartons (32 oz [900 mL] each) less-sodium, ready-to-use vegetable or chicken broth

1 cup (250 mL) water

2 cups (500 mL) sliced green beans

¼ cup (60 mL) golden miso

½ cup (125 mL) finely chopped parsley

Finely grated Parmesan cheese, for garnish

In a skillet over medium-high, heat oil, then add carrots, celery, and onion. Cook, stirring, until carrots are softened, about 7 minutes. Stir in thyme and pepper; add barley and stir to coat. Add 1 carton of the broth and bring to a boil. Transfer mixture to slow cooker. Add the remaining carton of broth and measured water. Cover slow cooker; cook on low for 6 to 8 hours. Add green beans and miso. Cover and cook on high for 15 minutes or until beans are tender. Sprinkle with parsley and serve topped with Parmesan cheese.

Makes 6 servings (1½ cups [375 mL] each).

Nutritional Information (per serving): Calories: 233, Protein: 8 g, Carbohydrate: 40 g, Fiber: 10 g, Sugars: 8 g, Fat: 5 g, Saturated Fat: 1 g, Trans Fat: 0 g, Cholesterol: 4 mg, Sodium: 804 mg, Potassium: 436 mg

BARLEY MINESTRONE

Talk about a meal in a soup bowl! This nourishing Italian-style vegetable soup is thick with slices of Italian sausage, a half-dozen vegetables, barley, and beans.

2 Tbsp (30 mL) canola oil

½ lb (250 g) Italian sausage (mild or hot), thinly sliced

1 large onion, chopped

1 garlic clove, minced

1 large celery stalk, thinly sliced

1 large carrot, diced

1 small green pepper, chopped

½ cup (125 mL) pot or pearl barley

2 Tbsp (30 mL) chopped parsley

½ tsp (2 mL) dried basil

1 bay leaf

¼ tsp (1 mL) salt

¼ tsp (1 mL) pepper

1 can (19 oz [540 mL]) diced tomatoes

1 carton (32 oz [900 mL]) less-sodium, ready-to-use chicken broth

2 cups (500 mL) water

1½ cups (375 mL) shredded cabbage

1 can (19 oz [540 mL]) kidney beans, drained

Freshly grated Parmesan cheese, for garnish

In a large saucepan or Dutch oven over medium-high, heat oil. Add sausage and lightly brown. Add onion, garlic, celery, carrot, and green pepper; cook until softened, about 5 minutes. Stir in barley, parsley, basil, bay leaf, salt, and pepper. Add tomatoes, broth, and water. Bring to a boil, then reduce heat; cover pan and simmer for 20 minutes. Add cabbage and kidney beans; cover pan and continue to simmer for an additional 30 minutes. Remove bay leaf and discard. Serve soup sprinkled with Parmesan cheese.

Makes 8 servings (1¼ cups [310 mL] each).

Nutritional Information (per serving): Calories: 301, Protein: 15 g, Carbohydrate: 28 g, Fiber: 7 g, Sugars: 5 g, Fat: 15 g, Saturated Fat: 4.5 g, Trans Fat: 0 g, Cholesterol: 38 mg, Sodium: 761 mg, Potassium: 238 mg

SAUSAGE, LENTIL, AND BARLEY SOUP

Italian sausages and green lentils pair with barley in this simple-to-make soup. Add bread, a green salad, and dessert to complete the meal.

2 tsp (10 mL) canola oil

2 mild or hot Italian sausages

5 celery stalks, including leaves

⅓ cup (75 mL) pot or pearl barley

⅓ cup (75 mL) dried green lentils

2 cartons (32 oz [900 mL] each) less-sodium, ready-to-use chicken broth, or 8 cups (2 L) water

¼ tsp (1 mL) pepper

In a large saucepan over medium-high, heat oil. Squeeze sausages out of their casings into the saucepan and cook, breaking up with a spoon, until no longer pink. Chop the celery, including leaves, and add to sausage. Cook, stirring, for 5 minutes. Stir in barley, lentils, and broth or water. Bring to a boil. Reduce heat, cover pan, and simmer for 45 minutes or until barley and lentils are tender. Season with pepper to taste.

Makes 6 servings (1⅔ cups [400 mL] each).

Nutritional Information (per serving): Calories: 171, Protein: 14 g, Carbohydrate: 17 g, Fiber: 4 g, Sugars: 3 g, Fat: 6 g, Saturated Fat: 1 g, Trans Fat: 0 g, Cholesterol: 23 mg, Sodium: 395 mg, Potassium: 204 mg

EASY BEEF BARLEY SOUP

Although it tastes like it has simmered for hours, this soup is made in just 30 minutes using pre-cooked and convenience products. The roast beef can be purchased cooked from a deli. The beef broth is canned and the barley is the quick-cooking variety.

1 Tbsp (15 mL) canola oil

½ cup (125 mL) chopped carrot

½ cup (125 mL) sliced celery

1 small onion, chopped

3 cans (10 oz [284 mL] each) condensed beef broth, undiluted

3½ cups (875 mL) water

2 cups (500 mL) chopped cooked roast beef

1 can (14 oz [398 mL]) diced tomatoes

1 cup (250 mL) quick-cooking barley (see Barley Bit)

1 tsp (5 mL) salt

½ tsp (2 mL) pepper

1 tsp (5 mL) dried thyme

1 bay leaf

In a large pot or Dutch oven over medium-high, heat oil. Sauté carrot, celery, and onion for 5 minutes or until onion is transparent. Add the broth and measured water. Add the roast beef, tomatoes, barley, salt, pepper, thyme, and bay leaf. Bring to a boil. Reduce heat, cover pan, and simmer for 25 minutes, stirring occasionally. Remove bay leaf before serving.

Makes 10 servings (1¼ cups [310 mL] each).

Nutritional Information (per serving): Calories: 117, Protein: 11 g, Carbohydrate: 11 g, Fiber: 2 g, Sugars: 2 g, Fat: 3.5 g, Saturated Fat: 0.5 g, Trans Fat: 0 g, Cholesterol: 23 mg, Sodium: 664 mg, Potassium: 145 mg

Barley Bit: You can substitute ½ cup (125 mL) regular pearl or pot barley for quick-cooking barley, if desired. Just increase simmering time to 1 hour.

BARLEY, BEEF, AND BROCCOLI SOUP

Here's a heartwarming soup packed with nutritious lean ground beef, barley, broccoli, tomatoes, celery, zucchini, and mushrooms. A sprinkle of grated cheddar can be added as you serve it.

½ lb (250 g) lean ground beef

1 small onion, chopped

1 garlic clove, minced

½ cup (125 mL) pot or pearl barley

2 cartons (32 oz [900 mL] each) less-sodium, ready-to-use beef broth

1 bunch broccoli

2 large tomatoes

3 celery stalks

1 medium zucchini

1 can (10 oz [284 mL]) sliced mushrooms

1 tsp (5 mL) chili powder

¼ tsp (1 mL) salt

¼ tsp (1 mL) pepper

Grated cheddar cheese, for garnish (optional)

In a large pot or Dutch oven over medium-high heat, brown ground beef; add onion and garlic, and sauté for 3 minutes. Drain fat. Add barley and beef broth. Bring to a boil. Reduce heat, cover pan, and simmer for 20 minutes.

Meanwhile, chop broccoli, tomatoes, celery, and zucchini into bite-sized pieces. Add to barley mixture, along with mushrooms and chili powder. Bring to a boil. Reduce heat, cover pan, and simmer for 25 minutes, stirring occasionally. Season to taste with salt and pepper. Serve sprinkled with cheddar cheese, if desired.

Makes 6 servings (2 cups [500 mL] each).

Nutritional Information (per serving): Calories: 230, Protein: 18 g, Carbohydrate: 27 g, Fiber: 6 g, Sugars: 7 g, Fat: 6 g, Saturated Fat: 2 g, Trans Fat: 0.4 g, Cholesterol: 34 mg, Sodium: 413 mg, Potassium: 727 mg

HEARTY BISON BARLEY SOUP

Purchase ground bison, either fresh or frozen, and brown it with onion to make this comforting, hearty barley soup. Once cooked, the barley will continue to thicken the soup, so add more water or broth if it gets too thick. Complete the meal with a salad and crusty bread.

1 lb (500 g) ground bison

1 medium onion, finely chopped

1 cup (250 mL) pot or pearl barley

1 can (28 oz [796 mL]) diced tomatoes

2 cans (10 oz [284 mL] each) condensed less-sodium beef broth, undiluted

4 cups (1 L) water

4 carrots, finely chopped

3 celery stalks, finely chopped

1 bay leaf

½ tsp (2 mL) dried thyme

¼ tsp (1 mL) pepper

¼ cup (60 mL) chopped parsley

In a large saucepan over medium-high heat, brown bison, breaking it into chunks as it browns. Add onion and sauté for 5 minutes. Stir in barley, then add tomatoes, beef broth, water, carrots, celery, bay leaf, thyme, and pepper. Bring to a boil. Reduce heat, cover pan, and simmer for 1 hour, adding more water if the soup becomes too thick. Remove bay leaf. Stir in chopped parsley and serve.

Makes 8 servings (1¾ cups [425 mL] each).

Nutritional Information (per serving): Calories: 268, Protein: 16 g, Carbohydrate: 29 g, Fiber: 6 g, Sugars: 5 g, Fat: 10 g, Saturated Fat: 0.2 g, Trans Fat: 0 g, Cholesterol: 40 mg, Sodium: 310 mg, Potassium: 476 mg

LAMB BARLEY SOUP

Cubes of stewing lamb are browned and then simmered with onion, barley, leek, and root vegetables to make this tasty soup.

1 Tbsp (15 mL) canola oil

1 lb (500 g) lamb stew meat, cut into 1-inch (2.5 cm) cubes

1 medium onion, chopped

1 cup (250 mL) pot or pearl barley

1 leek, thoroughly washed and diced

1 cup (250 mL) diced rutabaga or parsnips

1 cup (250 mL) diced carrots

½ tsp (2 mL) salt

¼ tsp (1 mL) pepper

6 cups (1.5 L) less-sodium chicken broth

Chopped parsley, for garnish

In a large saucepan or Dutch oven over high, heat oil. Add lamb cubes and brown. Add onion and barley; stir and cook for 2 minutes. Add leek, rutabaga or parsnips, carrots, salt, pepper, and broth. Bring to a boil. Cover pan, reduce heat, and simmer for 1 hour or until lamb and barley are tender. To serve, ladle into bowls and sprinkle with chopped parsley.

Makes 6 servings (1½ cups [375 mL] each).

Nutritional Information (per serving): Calories: 298, Protein: 23 g, Carbohydrate: 35 g, Fiber: 7 g, Sugars: 5 g, Fat: 7 g, Saturated Fat: 2 g, Trans Fat: 0 g, Cholesterol: 54 mg, Sodium: 412 mg, Potassium: 510 mg

CREAMY HAM AND LEEK SOUP

Pat finds this the perfect soup to serve for lunch at a ski chalet or to winter skaters or hikers. Barley thickens and adds fiber to this "stick-to-the-ribs" creamy soup made of ham and leeks.

2 small leeks

2 small onions

3 carrots

2 celery stalks

1–2 garlic cloves

1 Tbsp (15 mL) canola oil

¾ cup (175 mL) pot or pearl barley

1 cup (250 mL) chopped cooked ham

2 Tbsp (30 mL) whole barley flour

8 cups (2 L) less-sodium chicken or vegetable broth, or water

¼ tsp (1 mL) pepper

2 egg yolks (optional)

½ cup (125 mL) cream or milk

Chopped parsley, for garnish

Cut leeks in half lengthwise and wash carefully. Chop leeks, onions, carrots, celery, and garlic. In a large saucepan over medium-high, heat oil. Sauté chopped vegetables and garlic until softened, about 5 minutes. Add barley and ham; continue cooking for 3 minutes. Stir in the flour, then gradually add broth or water and pepper. Bring to a boil. Reduce heat, cover pan, and simmer for 1 hour, adding more liquid if necessary. Remove from heat. If using egg yolks, mix into the cream or milk and stir into the soup. Heat, stirring constantly, until soup thickens, but do not boil. Serve sprinkled with parsley.

Makes 10 servings (1⅓ cups [325 mL] each).

Nutritional Information (per serving): Calories: 152, Protein: 8 g, Carbohydrate: 20 g, Fiber: 4 g, Sugars: 3 g, Fat: 5 g, Saturated Fat: 2 g, Trans Fat: 0 g, Cholesterol: 18 mg, Sodium: 264 mg, Potassium: 197 mg

HEARTY CHICKEN BARLEY SOUP

This mouthwatering soup is made with cubes of chicken, barley, carrots, celery, and onion simmered in chicken broth and seasoned with summer savory and thyme.

1 Tbsp (15 mL) canola oil

1½ lb (750 g) boneless, skinless chicken breasts or thighs, cubed

½ cup (125 mL) pearl or pot barley

1 can (10 oz [284 mL]) condensed less-sodium chicken broth, undiluted

4 cups (1 L) water

1 cup (250 mL) diced carrots

1 cup (250 mL) diced celery

½ cup (125 mL) chopped onion

¼ tsp (1 mL) dried summer savory

¼ tsp (1 mL) dried thyme

¼ tsp (1 mL) pepper

1 bay leaf

In a large pot or Dutch oven over medium-high, heat oil. Add chicken and lightly brown. Add the barley, chicken broth, water, carrots, celery, onion, summer savory, thyme, pepper, and bay leaf. Bring to a boil. Reduce heat, cover pan, and simmer for 1 hour or until vegetables and barley are tender. Remove bay leaf. Serve hot.

Makes 6 servings (1½ cups [375 mL] each).

Nutritional Information (per serving): Calories: 272, Protein: 36 g, Carbohydrate: 17 g, Fiber: 4 g, Sugars: 2 g, Fat: 6 g, Saturated Fat: 1.5 g, Trans Fat: 0 g, Cholesterol: 88 mg, Sodium: 134 mg, Potassium: 394 mg

BARLEY FISH CHOWDER

This yummy version of classic fish chowder is made with shrimp and salmon, then thickened with barley. Other meaty fish, such as cod or haddock, can be substituted for the salmon.

4 slices bacon, cut into ½-inch (1 cm) pieces

1 medium onion, finely chopped

2 medium carrots, thinly sliced

½ cup (125 mL) pot or pearl barley

1 can (28 oz [796 mL]) plum tomatoes

2 cans (10 oz [284 mL] each) condensed less-sodium chicken or vegetable broth, undiluted

2½ cups (625 mL) water

½ tsp (2 mL) dried thyme

½ lb (250 g) shrimp, peeled and deveined

1 lb (500 g) salmon fillets, skinned and cut into chunks (see Barley Bit)

¼ tsp (1 mL) salt

¼ tsp (1 mL) pepper

In a large saucepan or Dutch oven over medium-high heat, cook bacon until browned and crisp, 8 to 10 minutes. Remove all but 1 tablespoon (15 mL) of fat from the pan. Add onion and carrots. Cook, stirring occasionally, until softened, about 2 minutes. Stir in barley. Add tomatoes, broth, water, and thyme. Break the tomatoes up with a fork. Bring to a boil, then reduce heat to low. Cover pan and simmer for 45 to 50 minutes. Add shrimp and salmon and continue cooking for about 10 minutes or until shrimp and salmon are cooked. Season with salt and pepper.

Makes 6 servings (2 cups [500 mL] each).

Nutritional Information (per serving): Calories: 299, Protein: 28 g, Carbohydrate: 23 g, Fiber: 5 g, Sugars: 5 g, Fat: 10 g, Saturated Fat: 2.5 g, Trans Fat: 0 g, Cholesterol: 106 mg, Sodium: 884 mg, Potassium: 474 mg

Barley Bit: To remove the skin from a salmon fillet, place the fillet skin-side down on a cutting board. Hold the tail end tightly. With a knife, cut down through the flesh to the skin. Then, holding the loose skin tightly, continue to slide the knife between the skin and the flesh, removing the skin.

MAIN DISHES

BEEF AND BARLEY STEW

No fuss, no bother: A less tender cut of beef slowly simmers on the stove with barley and winter vegetables to produce a luscious, thick, flavorful stew.

1½ lb (750 g) boneless beef chuck or blade

1 Tbsp (15 mL) canola oil

1 medium onion, diced

1 garlic clove, minced

2 Tbsp (30 mL) tomato paste

½ cup (125 mL) pearl or pot barley

2 cans (10 oz [284 mL] each) condensed less-sodium beef broth, undiluted

1 cup (250 mL) water

1 Tbsp (15 mL) Worcestershire sauce

½ tsp (2 mL) dried thyme

1 bay leaf

1 medium turnip, diced

3 carrots, sliced

2 celery stalks, sliced

Salt and pepper, to taste

Cut beef into 1½-inch (4 cm) cubes. In a large pot over medium-high, heat oil; add beef and brown well on all sides. Remove browned beef to a bowl. Add onion to the pot and cook for 3 minutes. Stir in garlic and tomato paste; cook for 2 minutes. Add browned beef, barley, beef broth, water, and Worcestershire sauce; bring to a boil and reduce heat to simmer. Add the thyme, bay leaf, turnip, carrots, and celery; simmer for 1 to 1½ hours or until meat, barley, and vegetables are tender. Remove bay leaf. Season to taste with salt and pepper. Serve hot.

Makes 6 servings.

Nutritional Information (per serving): Calories: 401, Protein: 23 g, Carbohydrate: 22 g, Fiber: 5 g, Sugars: 5 g, Fat: 25 g, Saturated Fat: 9 g, Trans Fat: 0 g, Cholesterol: 83 mg, Sodium: 398 mg, Potassium: 633 mg

BEER-BRAISED BEEF ON A BED OF BARLEY

This filling meal is sure to satisfy even the hungriest of eaters. Accompany with a glass of your favorite India Pale Ale.

4 Tbsp (60 mL) canola oil, divided
2 large onions, thinly sliced
2 lb (1 kg) boneless beef blade steak, sliced ¼-inch (6 mm) thick
1 tsp (5 mL) salt
½ tsp (2 mL) pepper
⅓ cup (75 mL) whole barley flour
1 bay leaf
¼ tsp (1 mL) dried thyme
1 bottle or can (12 oz [341 mL]) beer
¾ cup (175 mL) pot or pearl barley
1 can (10 oz [284 mL]) condensed less-sodium beef broth, undiluted
1 cup (250 mL) water
Chopped parsley, for garnish

In a large skillet over medium-high, heat 1 tablespoon (15 mL) of the oil. Add onion slices and brown lightly. Remove to a separate dish. Add 2 tablespoons (30 mL) of the oil and half of the meat to the skillet; sprinkle with half of the salt and pepper, then brown. Sprinkle with about half of the flour; stir and remove to a heavy Dutch oven or large saucepan. Repeat with the remaining meat, salt, pepper, and flour. Spoon into the Dutch oven and top with browned onions. Add the bay leaf, thyme, and beer. Bring to a boil and cover pan. Reduce heat and simmer for 1½ hours or until the meat is tender. Once the meat is cooked, remove the bay leaf.

Meanwhile, in a medium saucepan over medium-high, heat the remaining oil. Stir in barley. Add beef broth and water and bring to a boil. Cover pan and reduce heat. Simmer for 40 to 45 minutes or until barley is tender. Spoon barley onto a serving plate and top with beef and onion mixture. Sprinkle with chopped parsley.

Makes 6 servings.

Nutritional Information (per serving): Calories: 438, Protein: 38 g, Carbohydrate: 32 g, Fiber: 6 g, Sugars: 3 g, Fat: 16 g, Saturated Fat: 4.5 g, Trans Fat: 0 g, Cholesterol: 68 mg, Sodium: 500 mg, Potassium: 717 mg

BARLEY AND BEEF MULLIGAN STEW

Three hours in the slow cooker produces this mouthwatering stew. Once it has cooked, other leftover cooked vegetables can be added. Serve with a salad of tossed greens and crusty bread or rolls.

1½ lb (750 g) lean ground beef

1 medium green pepper, chopped

1 medium onion, chopped

3 garlic cloves, minced

1 cup (250 mL) pot or pearl barley

1 can (10 oz [284 mL]) condensed less-sodium beef broth, undiluted

1¼ cups (310 mL) water

1 can (19 oz [540 mL]) whole tomatoes

1 cup (250 mL) corn kernels

1 Tbsp (15 mL) packed brown sugar

½ tsp (2 mL) salt, or to taste

¼ tsp (1 mL) ground black pepper

1 Tbsp (15 mL) vinegar

In a large skillet over medium-high heat, lightly brown beef. Add green pepper, onion, and garlic, and sauté for 1 minute. Pour mixture into slow cooker. Stir in barley and beef broth. Add measured water. Stir in tomatoes, corn, brown sugar, salt, pepper, and vinegar. Cover slow cooker and cook on high for 3 hours or until barley is soft.

Makes 6 servings.

Nutritional Information (per serving): Calories: 428, Protein: 27 g, Carbohydrate: 40 g, Fiber: 7 g, Sugars: 7 g, Fat: 18 g, Saturated Fat: 7 g, Trans Fat: 1 g, Cholesterol: 77 mg, Sodium: 705 mg, Potassium: 689 mg

Barley Bit: For a faster stew, leave ground beef, green pepper, onion, and garlic mixture in the skillet. Stir in barley, beef broth, water, tomatoes, corn, brown sugar, salt, pepper, and vinegar. Bring to a boil. Reduce heat; cover pan and simmer for 1 hour or until barley is tender, stirring occasionally.

EASY CABBAGE ROLL CASSEROLE

This casserole has all the flavor of cabbage rolls without the painstaking preparation. Shredded cabbage (consider buying pre-shredded from the produce department) is layered with a mixture of browned ground beef and barley in tomato sauce. It's served topped with sour cream and chopped green onions.

1½ lb (750 g) lean ground beef

1 medium onion, chopped

1 garlic clove, minced

½ cup (125 mL) pot or pearl barley

1 can (14 oz [398 mL]) tomato sauce

1⅔ cups (400 mL) water

½ tsp (2 mL) salt

¼ tsp (1 mL) pepper

4 cups (1 L) shredded cabbage

6 Tbsp (90 mL) sour cream

6 tsp (30 mL) chopped green onions

In a large skillet over medium-high heat, brown beef, onion, and garlic. Drain the fat. Stir in barley, then add tomato sauce, water, salt, and pepper. Bring to a boil; reduce heat, cover pan, and simmer for 30 minutes.

Preheat oven to 350°F (180°C). Grease an 8-cup (2 L) casserole dish.

Place half the cabbage in the dish. Layer it with half the barley beef mixture. Repeat layers. Cover dish and bake for 45 minutes. Top each serving with 1 tablespoon (15 mL) of the sour cream and 1 teaspoon (5 mL) of the green onions.

Makes 6 servings.

Nutritional Information (per serving): Calories: 345, Protein: 27 g, Carbohydrate: 23 g, Fiber: 5 g, Sugars: 6 g, Fat: 18 g, Saturated Fat: 7 g, Trans Fat: 0.5 g, Cholesterol: 68 mg, Sodium: 1124 mg, Potassium: 390 mg

RUSTIC ITALIAN PORK STEW WITH BARLEY

Morsels of boneless pork loin are slowly simmered with mushrooms and carrots in a tomato sauce spiked with cinnamon, raisins, and a splash of wine vinegar. The stew is spooned over cooked barley, which absorbs the flavorful sauce.

2 cups (500 mL) pot or pearl barley

4 cups (1 L) chicken broth

1 lb (500 g) boneless pork loin, cut into 1-inch (2.5 cm) cubes

1 Tbsp (15 mL) canola oil

1 large onion, coarsely chopped

2 carrots, sliced

8 oz (250 g) fresh mushrooms, coarsely chopped

1 can (7.5 oz [213 mL]) tomato sauce

1 cup (250 mL) dry red wine or chicken broth

1 tsp (5 mL) dried thyme

¾ tsp (4 mL) dried oregano

¼ tsp (1 mL) ground cinnamon

¼ tsp (1 mL) salt

Freshly ground black pepper, to taste

½ cup (125 mL) raisins

2 Tbsp (30 mL) red wine vinegar

In a large saucepan over high heat, bring barley and chicken broth to a boil. Reduce heat; cover pan and simmer for 45 minutes. Meanwhile, in a large skillet over medium heat, brown pork in canola oil, stirring occasionally. Stir in onion, carrots, and mushrooms, and cook for 2 minutes. Add tomato sauce, wine or broth, thyme, oregano, cinnamon, salt, and pepper. Bring to a boil; reduce heat and stir in raisins and red wine vinegar. Cover pan and simmer for 25 minutes. Serve over cooked barley.

Makes 6 servings.

Nutritional Information (per serving): Calories: 539, Protein: 32 g, Carbohydrate: 72 g, Fiber: 14 g, Sugars: 15 g, Fat: 11 g, Saturated Fat: 3 g, Trans Fat: 0 g, Cholesterol: 61 mg, Sodium: 621 mg, Potassium: 820 mg

VEGETABLE AND PORK FRIED BARLEY

This tasty stir-fry can be made with cooked pork or chicken. It's a great way to use up leftovers. To cut the preparation time, pre-cook the barley and refrigerate until ready to use.

1 cup (250 mL) pot or pearl barley

1 can (10 oz [284 mL]) condensed less-sodium chicken broth, undiluted

1 cup (250 mL) water

1 Tbsp (15 mL) canola oil

2 carrots, thinly sliced

1 cup (250 mL) diced zucchini

2 celery stalks, sliced

1½ cups (375 mL) diced cooked pork or chicken

1 small sweet red pepper, diced

2 eggs, lightly beaten

1 cup (250 mL) bean sprouts

3 Tbsp (45 mL) oyster sauce

3 Tbsp (45 mL) light soy sauce

2 Tbsp (30 mL) rice vinegar

In a medium saucepan over high heat, combine barley, chicken broth, and water; bring to a boil. Reduce heat; cover pan and simmer for 45 minutes, stirring partway through. If necessary, drain excess liquid.

In a large non-stick skillet over high, heat canola oil; stir-fry carrots, zucchini, and celery for 2 minutes. Add cooked barley and stir-fry for 1 minute. Add pork and red pepper; stir-fry for 1 minute. Make a well in the mixture and pour in eggs; stir-fry for 30 seconds, then stir in bean sprouts and continue to stir-fry until eggs are cooked.

In a small bowl, stir together oyster sauce, soy sauce, and rice vinegar. Stir sauce into stir-fry and serve.

Makes 4 servings.

Nutritional Information (per serving): Calories: 412, Protein: 31 g, Carbohydrate: 50 g, Fiber: 10 g, Sugars: 5 g, Fat: 11 g, Saturated Fat: 2.5 g, Trans Fat: 0 g, Cholesterol: 153 mg, Sodium: 1007 mg, Potassium: 504 mg

BARLEY AND APRICOT STUFFED PORK TENDERLOIN

A dinner guest pleaser, this stuffed pork tenderloin tastes as impressive as it looks. A medley of hearty winter vegetables can be roasted at the same time for a colorful and delicious side dish. Or serve with green beans.

2 tsp (10 mL) canola oil

3 Tbsp (45 mL) chopped onion

¼ cup (60 mL) pot or pearl barley

1 cup (250 mL) less-sodium chicken broth

¼ cup (60 mL) slivered almonds

⅓ cup (75 mL) dried apricots, diced

1 Tbsp (15 mL) chopped parsley

¼ tsp (1 mL) dried thyme

2 large pork tenderloins (about 1 lb [500 g] each)

Salt, to taste

Pepper, to taste

Preheat oven to 350°F (180°C).

In a medium saucepan over medium-high, heat oil. Add onion and sauté until softened, about 2 minutes. Stir in barley and chicken broth. Bring to a boil; cover pan and reduce heat to simmer for 40 minutes. Meanwhile, spread almonds on a baking sheet. Bake for 5 to 10 minutes or until golden. Allow cooked barley to cool, then stir in almonds, apricots, parsley, and thyme.

Return oven to 350°F (180°C). Slice tenderloins down the center, cutting just slightly more than halfway through. Sprinkle with salt and pepper. Spoon barley stuffing down the center of each tenderloin. Place tenderloins on a rack in a roasting pan and roast in the oven for 50 to 60 minutes or until a meat thermometer inserted into the tenderloins registers 160°F (70°C). Excess stuffing can be spooned into a small baking dish and baked for the last 30 minutes, to serve as a side. Slice each tenderloin into 3 portions and serve.

Makes 6 servings.

Nutritional Information (per serving): Calories: 273, Protein: 34 g, Carbohydrate: 12 g, Fiber: 2 g, Sugars: 1 g, Fat: 9 g, Saturated Fat: 2 g, Trans Fat: 0 g, Cholesterol: 99 mg, Sodium: 202 mg, Potassium: 662 mg

LAMB BRAISED WITH ARTICHOKES, OLIVES, AND BARLEY

The flavors of the sunny Mediterranean are captured in this barley skillet dish. Delight in the lamb, artichokes, and olives seasoned with oregano.

2 Tbsp (30 mL) olive oil

1 lb (500 g) lamb stew meat, cut into 1-inch (2.5 cm) cubes

1 small onion, chopped

1 garlic clove, minced

¾ cup (175 mL) pot or pearl barley

2½ cups (625 mL) less-sodium chicken or vegetable broth

1 can (14 oz [398 mL]) artichokes, drained and halved

1 can (7 oz [200 mL]) pitted and sliced olives, drained

¼ tsp (1 mL) dried oregano

¼ tsp (1 mL) pepper

In a large skillet over medium-high, heat oil. Add lamb and cook until browned, about 5 minutes. Add onion and garlic. Stir in barley and broth. Bring to a boil; cover pan and reduce heat. Simmer for 45 minutes, stirring halfway through. Stir in artichokes, olives, oregano, and pepper. Cook for 15 minutes until artichokes and olives are hot.

Makes 4 servings.

Nutritional Information (per serving): Calories. 424, Protein: 31 g, Carbohydrate: 38 g, Fiber: 7 g, Sugars: 2 g, Fat: 16 g, Saturated Fat: 4 g, Trans Fat: 0 g, Cholesterol: 77 mg, Sodium: 528 mg, Potassium: 460 mg

LAMB AND VEGETABLE BARLEY HOT POT

This barley casserole is packed full of succulent lamb and hearty vegetables. You'll want to serve it with crusty bread and a soup spoon to enjoy the flavorful broth.

1 Tbsp (15 mL) canola oil

4 lamb chops

1 small onion, cut into quarters lengthwise

½ small butternut squash

½ rutabaga

2 small leeks, cut into 1-inch (2.5 cm) pieces

½ cup (125 mL) pot or pearl barley

1 carton (32 oz [900 mL]) less-sodium, ready-to-use vegetable or chicken broth, heated

1 bay leaf

¼ tsp (1 mL) dried thyme

¼ tsp (1 mL) pepper

Chopped parsley, for garnish

Preheat oven to 325°F (160°C).

In a large skillet over high, heat oil. Add the lamb chops and sear on both sides. Transfer chops to a large casserole dish.

Add the onions to the skillet. Reduce the heat to medium-high and cook for 5 minutes or until slightly browned. Meanwhile, peel the squash. Remove and discard seeds and cut squash into 1-inch (2.5 cm) chunks. Peel the rutabaga and cut into sticks. Stir the squash, rutabaga, and leeks into the onions. Sprinkle in the barley. Pour in the broth. Add the bay leaf, thyme, and pepper. Stir and cook for 2 minutes, then spoon over lamb chops in the casserole dish. Cover and cook in the oven for 1 hour or until the vegetables and barley are tender. Let stand for 10 minutes. Remove bay leaf and discard. Sprinkle casserole with parsley and serve.

Makes 4 servings.

Nutritional Information (per serving): Calories: 287, Protein: 18 g, Carbohydrate: 37 g, Fiber: 7 g, Sugars: 7 g, Fat: 8 g, Saturated Fat: 1.5 g, Trans Fat: 0 g, Cholesterol: 43 mg, Sodium: 196 mg, Potassium: 502 mg

BARLEY JAMBALAYA

Louisiana flavors are captured in this skillet-simmered, well-seasoned combination of spicy sausage, chicken, shrimp, and barley.

1 lb (500 g) hot or mild Italian sausage, sliced

1 boneless, skinless chicken breast, cut into bite-sized pieces

1 small onion, finely chopped

2 garlic cloves, minced

1 tsp (5 mL) dried oregano

1 tsp (5 mL) chili powder

1 cup (250 mL) pot or pearl barley

1 can (28 oz [796 mL]) diced tomatoes

1 can (10 oz [284 mL]) condensed less-sodium chicken broth, undiluted

1¼ cups (310 mL) water

8 oz (250 g) peeled and deveined shrimp, cooked

1 Tbsp (15 mL) chopped parsley

In a large non-stick skillet over medium-high heat, cook sausage and chicken until no longer pink, 6 to 8 minutes. Drain fat from the pan. Reduce heat to medium. Add onions and cook until soft. Add garlic, oregano, and chili powder; cook for 1 minute. Stir in barley, tomatoes, chicken broth, and water. Bring to a boil, reduce heat, cover pan, and simmer for 40 minutes. Add shrimp and cook for 10 minutes. Stir in parsley and serve.

Makes 8 servings.

Nutritional Information (per serving): Calories: 374, Protein: 21 g, Carbohydrate: 26 g, Fiber: 5 g, Sugars: 3 g, Fat: 21 g, Saturated Fat: 7 g, Trans Fat: 0 g, Cholesterol: 105 mg, Sodium: 765 mg, Potassium: 314 mg

CHORIZO AND KALE SAUTÉ WITH CANNELLINI BEANS

Only six ingredients are needed to make this colorful, hearty meal. If the sausage doesn't provide enough spice for your taste, sprinkle lightly with red pepper flakes.

1 cup (250 mL) water

Pinch of salt

¼ cup (60 mL) pot or pearl barley

¾ lb (375 g) chorizo or Andouille sausage

4 sun-dried tomatoes, halved and thinly sliced (see Barley Bit)

2 garlic cloves, minced, or to taste

4 cups (1 L) thinly sliced kale leaves, stems and ribs removed

1 can (19 oz [540 mL]) cannellini (white kidney) or Romano beans, drained

In a medium saucepan over high heat, bring water and salt to a boil. Add barley; return to a boil, then cover pan and reduce heat. Simmer for 40 minutes.

Heat a large non-stick skillet. Meanwhile, dice sausage and then toss it into the pan, stirring to brown lightly. Add sun-dried tomatoes to the skillet. Then stir in garlic and sauté briefly. Add kale to skillet along with cooked barley and cannellini or Romano beans; cook until kale is slightly wilted.

Makes 4 servings.

Nutritional Information (per serving): Calories: 600, Protein: 33 g, Carbohydrate: 43 g, Fiber: 10 g, Sugars: 5 g, Fat: 33 g, Saturated Fat: 12 g, Trans Fat: 0 g, Cholesterol: 75 mg, Sodium: 1601 mg, Potassium: 911 mg

Barley Bit: If the sun-dried tomatoes are very firm, soak for several minutes in warm water, then drain and thinly slice.

SWEET AND SOUR CHICKEN BARLEY CASSEROLE

Chicken, onion, celery, red pepper, barley, and pineapple chunks are slowly baked in a sweet and sour sauce. A garnish of cooked snow peas is added just before serving.

3 Tbsp (45 mL) canola oil, divided

2 lb (1 kg) boneless, skinless chicken pieces

1 small onion

2 celery stalks

1 sweet red pepper

1 cup (250 mL) pot or pearl barley

1 can (14 oz [398 mL]) pineapple chunks, drained, reserving juice

¼ cup (60 mL) packed brown sugar

2 Tbsp (30 mL) cornstarch

¼ cup (60 mL) rice or white vinegar

¼ cup (60 mL) soy sauce

2 cups (500 mL) less-sodium chicken broth

1 cup (250 mL) snow peas, cooked

Preheat oven to 350°F (180°C).

In a large skillet over medium-high, heat 2 tablespoons (30 mL) of the oil. Brown chicken pieces and transfer to a large casserole dish. Meanwhile, chop onion, celery, and red pepper into medium chunks. Add the remaining oil to skillet along with vegetables. Stir for 2 minutes. Spoon vegetables, barley, and pineapple over chicken.

In a medium saucepan, combine brown sugar, cornstarch, vinegar, and soy sauce. Bring to a boil over medium-high heat, then add chicken broth and reserved pineapple juice. Bring to a boil and simmer for 3 minutes. Remove from heat and pour over chicken. Cover and bake for 1½ hours. Serve garnished with cooked snow peas.

Makes 6 servings.

Nutritional Information (per serving): Calories: 491, Protein: 40 g, Carbohydrate: 54 g, Fiber: 7 g, Sugars: 23 g, Fat: 13 g, Saturated Fat: 3 g, Trans Fat: 0 g, Cholesterol: 89 mg, Sodium: 1036 mg, Potassium: 284 mg

SLOW COOKER CHICKEN BARLEY CHILI

Preparing a meal doesn't get easier. Just combine all these chili ingredients in a slow cooker and look forward to a flavorful dinner. The chili is mild, so add additional chili powder if desired.

1 lb (500 g) boneless, skinless chicken breasts or thighs, cut into bite-sized pieces

1 can (19 oz [540 mL]) pinto or black beans, drained

1 can (12 oz [341 mL]) corn kernels, drained

1 cup (250 mL) pot or pearl barley

4 cups (1 L) water

1 can (28 oz [796 mL]) diced tomatoes

1 can (7.5 oz [213 mL]) tomato sauce

1 Tbsp (15 mL) chili powder, or to taste

1 tsp (5 mL) ground cumin

1 tsp (5 mL) dried oregano

Cheddar cheese, sour cream, cucumbers, lettuce, green onions, tortilla chips (optional)

In a slow cooker, combine chicken, beans, corn, barley, water, tomatoes, tomato sauce, chili powder, cumin, and oregano. Cover and cook on low for 6 to 8 hours or on high for 4 to 6 hours, stirring once halfway through cooking time, especially around the bottom edges. Add more water, if required. Serve garnished with grated cheddar cheese, sour cream, diced cucumbers and lettuce, sliced green onions, and tortilla chips (if using).

Makes 6 servings.

Nutritional Information (per serving, excluding garnishes): Calories: 339, Protein: 25 g, Carbohydrate: 49 g, Fiber: 10 g, Sugars: 8 g, Fat: 4 g, Saturated Fat: 1 g, Trans Fat: 0 g, Cholesterol: 44 mg, Sodium: 1007 mg, Potassium: 552 mg

ASPARAGUS, CHICKEN, AND MUSHROOM RISOTTO

Risotto is such satisfying comfort food and so effortless to make with barley. This recipe calls for a minimum of stirring and is made with pieces of chicken, pre-sliced mushrooms, and asparagus.

2 Tbsp (30 mL) canola oil, divided

1 lb (500 g) boneless, skinless chicken breasts, cubed

7 oz (200 g) sliced mushrooms

1 small onion, finely diced

1 cup (250 mL) pot or pearl barley

1 carton (32 oz [900 mL]) less-sodium, ready-to-use chicken broth

½ lb (250 g) asparagus, trimmed

¼ cup (60 mL) grated Parmesan cheese, for garnish

In a large skillet over medium-high, heat half of the oil. Sauté chicken breasts and mushrooms until chicken is browned. Remove from pan. Add remaining oil to the pan along with the onion and sauté until softened. Stir in barley, then chicken broth, and bring to a boil. Reduce heat; cover pan and simmer for 25 minutes. Stir vigorously for 15 seconds. Stir in cooked chicken and mushrooms and simmer for 15 minutes. Cut asparagus stalks into thirds and stir into barley mixture. Continue to simmer for another 10 minutes. Sprinkle with Parmesan cheese just before serving.

Makes 4 servings.

Nutritional Information (per serving): Calories: 456, Protein: 39 g, Carbohydrate: 46 g, Fiber: 10 g, Sugars: 4 g, Fat: 14 g, Saturated Fat: 4 g, Trans Fat: 0 g, Cholesterol: 75 mg, Sodium: 258 mg, Potassium: 330 mg

CURRIED CHICKEN AND BARLEY

The mouthwatering aroma of a mild curry greets you when you lift the lid of the slow cooker containing this combination of chicken and barley. The final addition of yogurt makes the sauce extra creamy. Serve with a green vegetable.

2 lb (1 kg) boneless, skinless chicken thighs (about 12)

3 Tbsp (45 mL) freshly squeezed lemon juice

1 Tbsp (15 mL) canola oil

4 celery stalks, coarsely diced

1 medium onion, chopped

2 garlic cloves, minced

1 Tbsp (15 mL) minced fresh ginger

2 Tbsp (30 mL) curry powder

½ tsp (2 mL) salt

1 cup (250 mL) pot or pearl barley

1 cup (250 mL) less-sodium chicken broth

1 can (28 oz [796 mL]) diced tomatoes

1 cup (250 mL) full fat plain yogurt

Parsley, for garnish (optional)

Sprinkle chicken with lemon juice; arrange at bottom of slow cooker. In a large skillet over medium, heat oil; add celery and onions. Cook, stirring, for 5 minutes until celery is softened. Add garlic and ginger; stir and cook for 1 minute. Add curry powder and salt; stir and cook for 1 more minute. Stir in barley and then add chicken broth and tomatoes; bring to a boil and pour over chicken.

Cover slow cooker and cook on low for 5 to 6 hours or on high for 2½ to 3 hours, until a food thermometer inserted into the chicken registers 165°F (74°C). Stir yogurt into chicken mixture. Cover and cook on high for 10 minutes. Garnish with parsley, if desired, and serve.

Makes 6 servings.

Nutritional Information (per serving): Calories: 433, Protein: 33 g, Carbohydrate: 38 g, Fiber: 8 g, Sugars: 7 g, Fat: 18 g, Saturated Fat: 5 g, Trans Fat: 0 g, Cholesterol: 128 mg, Sodium: 647 mg, Potassium: 300 mg

SEAFOOD KEBABS ON BARLEY

Cooked barley flecked with chopped parsley makes a flavor-absorbing bed for grilled or broiled seafood, such as these seafood kebabs. To glam up this dish, serve the kebabs over Lemon Parmesan Barley (p. 141). The skewers are threaded with shrimp, scallops, bacon, and peppers, then basted with a mixture of olive oil, lemon juice, and a bit of dried thyme.

⅔ cup (150 mL) pot or pearl barley

1 can (10 oz [284 mL]) condensed less-sodium chicken broth, undiluted

1¼ cups (310 mL) water

¼ cup (60 mL) chopped parsley

¼ cup (60 mL) lemon juice

2 Tbsp (30 mL) olive oil

¼ tsp (1 mL) dried thyme

¼ tsp (1 mL) pepper

½ small green pepper, cut into 1-inch (2.5 cm) squares

½ small yellow pepper, cut into 1-inch (2.5 cm) squares

12 medium scallops

4 thick slices bacon, cut into thirds

12 large raw shrimp, peeled

If using wooden skewers, soak in water for several hours.

In a medium saucepan over high heat, bring barley, chicken broth, and water to a boil; cover pan and reduce heat. Simmer until barley is tender, about 50 minutes. Stir in parsley.

Meanwhile, preheat barbecue to medium-high. In a small bowl, combine lemon juice, oil, thyme, and pepper. Thread green pepper, yellow pepper, scallops, bacon, and shrimp onto 4 metal or long wooden skewers, alternating items and beginning and ending with peppers. Brush with lemon mixture. Grill for about 10 to 12 minutes, or until shrimp, scallops, and bacon are cooked, turning once. (Alternately, place on rack in broiler pan and broil for 10 minutes, or until cooked, turning once.) Spoon barley onto 4 plates and top with kebabs.

Makes 4 servings.

Nutritional Information (per serving): Calories: 407, Protein: 16 g, Carbohydrate: 30 g, Fiber: 6 g, Sugars: 1 g, Fat: 25 g, Saturated Fat: 7 g, Trans Fat: 0 g, Cholesterol: 68 mg, Sodium: 612 mg, Potassium: 337 mg

SPINACH, SMOKED SALMON, AND BARLEY RISOTTO

This flavor-packed risotto is divine! Smaller servings of this very colorful barley risotto also make a great appetizer. Be sure not to overcook the spinach.

1 Tbsp (15 mL) olive oil

1 small onion, finely chopped

1 garlic clove, finely chopped

1 cup (250 mL) pot or pearl barley

⅓ cup (75 mL) dry white wine or water

1 carton (32 oz [900 mL]) less-sodium, ready-to-use chicken broth

6 oz (170 g) smoked salmon, cut into strips

6 oz (170 g) baby spinach, cut into smaller pieces

1 cup (250 mL) grated Parmesan cheese

2 tsp (10 mL) lemon juice

In a large skillet over medium-high, heat oil. Add onion and garlic and sauté for 2 to 3 minutes. Add barley, stirring until well coated. Add wine or water and cook until liquid has almost evaporated, about 1 to 2 minutes. Add broth and bring to a boil. Reduce heat; cover pan and simmer for 45 to 55 minutes or until barley is tender, stirring vigorously halfway through for 15 seconds. Stir in salmon and then add spinach; cover pan and simmer until spinach is barely wilted, about 5 minutes. Gently stir in cheese and lemon juice.

Makes 4 servings.

Nutritional Information (per serving): Calories: 514, Protein: 44 g, Carbohydrate: 47 g, Fiber: 10 g, Sugars: 2 g, Fat: 16 g, Saturated Fat: 6 g, Trans Fat: 0 g, Cholesterol: 107 mg, Sodium: 525 mg, Potassium: 618 mg

SHRIMP AND PEA BARLEY RISOTTO

Barley cooks to a creamy risotto without all of the stirring. Use medium-sized shrimp and fresh peas when they're in season.

1 Tbsp (15 mL) olive oil

1 small onion, finely diced

2 garlic cloves, minced

1 tsp (5 mL) grated lemon rind

¼ tsp (1 mL) pepper

1 cup (250 mL) pot or pearl barley

4 cups (1 L) less-sodium chicken broth

12 oz (350 g) peeled and deveined raw shrimp

1 cup (250 mL) fresh or frozen peas

2 Tbsp (30 mL) chopped fresh parsley, or sprigs of fresh mint

In a large saucepan over medium-high, heat oil. Stir in onion, garlic, lemon rind, and pepper, and sauté until onion is softened, about 3 minutes. Stir in barley and broth; bring to a boil. Reduce heat; cover pan and simmer for 45 minutes, stirring vigorously halfway through for 15 seconds. Stir in shrimp and peas; cover pan and simmer until shrimp are pink and peas are tender, about 5 minutes. Sprinkle with parsley or garnish with mint and serve.

Makes 4 servings.

Nutritional Information (per serving): Calories: 358, Protein: 29 g, Carbohydrate: 48 g, Fiber: 10 g, Sugars: 4 g, Fat: 6 g, Saturated Fat: 1 g, Trans Fat: 0 g, Cholesterol: 119 mg, Sodium: 312 mg, Potassium: 236 mg

CREAM BARLEY WITH TOMATOES AND MUSHROOMS

This toothsome vegetarian casserole is packed with protein. A salad and bread will complete the meal.

4 cups (1 L) water

2 cups (500 mL) pot or pearl barley

2 Tbsp (30 mL) butter

2 garlic cloves, minced

1 medium onion, sliced

½ lb (250 g) fresh mushrooms, sliced (about 3¾ cups [925 mL])

1 can (14 oz [398 mL]) diced tomatoes

⅓ cup (75 mL) pitted black olives, chopped

1 tsp (5 mL) dried basil

1 cup (250 mL) sour cream

½ cup (125 mL) grated Parmesan cheese

1 cup (250 mL) grated cheddar or mozzarella cheese

2 medium tomatoes, sliced

¼ cup (60 mL) dry breadcrumbs

Sprig of fresh thyme (optional)

In a large pot over high heat, bring the water to a boil. Stir in barley; reduce heat, cover pan, and simmer for 40 minutes.

Preheat oven to 350°F (180°C).

Meanwhile, in a medium skillet over medium heat, melt butter; add garlic, onion, and mushrooms and sauté until onion is soft and liquid has evaporated, about 5 minutes.

In a large bowl, combine cooked onion mixture with cooked barley, canned tomatoes, olives, basil, sour cream, Parmesan cheese, and half of the cheddar or mozzarella cheese. Spoon into an ungreased 8-cup (2 L) casserole dish. Place sliced tomatoes around the edge of the dish. Sprinkle with remaining cheese and breadcrumbs. Bake for 40 minutes or until browned. If desired, serve garnished with fresh thyme.

Makes 8 servings.

Nutritional Information (per serving): Calories: 389, Protein: 14 g, Carbohydrate: 49 g, Fiber: 9 g, Sugars: 5 g, Fat: 16 g, Saturated Fat: 9 g, Trans Fat: 0.1 g, Cholesterol: 47 mg, Sodium: 382 mg, Potassium: 358 mg

MUSHROOM BARLEY BURGERS

Fire up the grill! These vegetarian barley burgers are simple and easy to make. Serve in buns and top with salsa or wasabi stirred into mayonnaise, as well as lettuce, sliced tomatoes, and onions. You can also add a slice of cheese while browning the second side.

1 cup (250 mL) pot or pearl barley

3 cups (750 mL) water

2 Tbsp (30 mL) canola oil, divided

1 small onion, finely chopped

1 garlic clove, finely chopped

1 small carrot, finely chopped

½ lb (250 g) mushrooms, chopped

2 Tbsp (30 mL) chopped parsley

1 tsp (5 mL) grated lemon rind

1 tsp (5 mL) salt

½ tsp (2 mL) pepper

2 cups (500 mL) fresh breadcrumbs, divided

In a medium saucepan over high heat, combine barley and water; bring to a boil. Reduce heat and cover pan; simmer for 45 to 50 minutes or until barley is tender. If necessary, drain any excess water. Spread in a shallow dish to cool. In a large skillet over medium-high, heat half of the oil. Add onion, garlic, and carrot; stir and cook for 3 minutes or until vegetables are tender. Add mushrooms and cook until any liquid evaporates. Add parsley, lemon rind, salt, and pepper. Combine mixture with barley. Stir in ½ cup (125 mL) of the breadcrumbs. Place in a food processor and process until mixture holds together but you can still see some of the barley. On a plastic-wrap-lined tray or baking sheet, spoon mixture into 6 portions; shape into patties and coat with remaining breadcrumbs. In a large skillet over medium-high, heat the remaining oil and cook burgers 5 minutes per side or until browned and crisp. Alternately, heat the barbecue to medium-high and generously spray the grill with oil. Barbecue for 5 minutes per side.

Makes 6 burger patties.

Nutritional Information (per patty): Calories: 215, Protein: 6 g, Carbohydrate: 37 g, Fiber: 7 g, Sugars: 3 g, Fat: 6 g, Saturated Fat: 0.5 g, Trans Fat: 0 g, Cholesterol: 0 mg, Sodium: 486 mg, Potassium: 286 mg

ZUCCHINI, BARLEY, AND BULGAR STUFFED TOMATOES

The wholesome filling of barley, bulgar, and almonds makes this vegetarian main dish equally delicious when made with garden fresh or winter tomatoes. Serve it with a traditional ale.

1 Tbsp (15 mL) canola oil

1 small onion, chopped

¾ cup (175 mL) pot or pearl barley

3 cups (750 mL) less-sodium chicken or vegetable broth

¾ cup (175 mL) whole grain bulgar

1 cup (250 mL) chopped zucchini

⅓ cup (75 mL) toasted sliced almonds

1 tsp (5 mL) dried thyme

6 very large beefsteak tomatoes (or 8 large tomatoes)

½ cup (125 mL) grated white cheddar cheese

In a large saucepan over medium-high, heat oil and add onion. Sauté until onion is softened, about 3 to 4 minutes. Stir in barley. Add broth, then bring to a boil. Reduce heat, cover pan, and simmer for 30 minutes. Stir in bulgar and continue to simmer for 12 to 15 minutes or until grains are almost tender. Add zucchini; cover pan and cook for an additional 3 to 5 minutes, or until zucchini is cooked but still firm. Remove from heat and stir in almonds and thyme.

Meanwhile, preheat oven to 375°F (190°C).

Cut a thin slice from the stem ends of the tomatoes; using a small knife and spoon, scoop out centers. Sprinkle cavities lightly with salt and place cut side down on towel to drain, about 5 minutes. Fill tomato cavities with stuffing, packing firmly; sprinkle with cheese. Place on a baking sheet and bake for about 15 minutes or until tomato skin is wilted and cheese is golden brown.

Makes 6 servings.

Nutritional Information (per serving): Calories: 299, Protein: 13 g, Carbohydrate: 46 g, Fiber: 11 g, Sugars: 8 g, Fat: 9 g, Saturated Fat: 2.5 g, Trans Fat: 0 g, Cholesterol: 13 mg, Sodium: 153 mg, Potassium: 825 mg

MAIN DISHES

BASIC PIZZA CRUST

Barley flour combined with white flour makes this rustic pizza crust.

1 cup (250 mL) lukewarm water

1 Tbsp (15 mL) granulated sugar

1 envelope (¼ oz [8 g]) regular dry yeast (2¼ tsp [11 mL])

1 Tbsp (15 mL) olive oil

1½ tsp (7 mL) salt

1½ cups (375 mL) whole barley flour

1½ cups (375 mL) all-purpose flour

Cornmeal, for sprinkling

In a large mixing bowl, combine water, sugar, and yeast. Let rest for about 10 minutes to proof the yeast. Stir in oil, salt, barley flour, and all-purpose flour, mixing well. Add a little more flour if dough is sticky. Turn the dough out of the bowl onto a lightly floured surface and knead vigorously until smooth and elastic. Place the ball of dough in a greased bowl; cover with a damp cloth and let dough rise until doubled in bulk, approximately 1¼ hours. Punch down the ball of dough and turn it out onto a lightly floured surface. Let dough rest for 15 minutes. Preheat oven to 425°F (220°C).

Grease a pizza pan and sprinkle with cornmeal. Roll out dough into a ½-inch (1 cm) thick circle the same diameter as the pan and place on pan. Or place dough on pan and pat it out into a ½- inch (1 cm) thick crust, being careful not to leave it thicker in the center.

To complete the pizza, top crust with ½ cup (125 mL) to ¾ cup (175 mL) sauce and your favorite toppings, including cheese. Bake on middle rack for 15 to 25 minutes or until edges of crust are golden and cheese is bubbly.

Makes one 12-inch (30 cm) pizza crust.

Nutritional Information (whole crust, without sauce or toppings): Calories: 1457, Protein: 23 g, Carbohydrate: 282 g, Fiber: 28 g, Sugars: 17 g, Fat: 41 g, Saturated Fat: 2.5 g, Trans Fat: 0 g, Cholesterol: 0 g, Sodium: 3574 mg, Potassium: 327 mg

SIDES

BARLEY AND MUSHROOM CASSEROLE

Any kind of mushrooms or a mixture of them can be used in this dish, which Linda's mom always makes. We've indicated how to cook the casserole in the oven, but if you need to free up oven space, it can be cooked in a slow cooker on low for 3 to 4 hours or in a rice cooker for one cycle. It can be garnished with cashew nuts, if desired. And it's delicious with barbecued burgers, steaks, ribs, or chicken, or as part of a comfort food dinner.

2 Tbsp (30 mL) canola oil

1 medium onion, chopped

¾ lb (375 g) fresh mushrooms, sliced

1½ cups (375 mL) pot or pearl barley

3 cups (750 mL) beef broth or bouillon

Salt and pepper, to taste

Preheat oven to 350°F (180°C).

In a large skillet over medium-high, heat oil and add onion. Sauté until transparent, about 5 minutes. Add mushrooms and continue cooking for about 5 minutes. Add barley and sauté until lightly browned, about 5 minutes. Remove barley mixture to a 1½-quart (1.5 L) casserole dish. Add the broth or bouillon and season with salt and pepper. Cover and bake for 1½ hours.

Makes 6 servings.

Nutritional Information (per serving): Calories: 243, Protein: 8 g, Carbohydrate: 42 g, Fiber: 9 g, Sugars: 2 g, Fat: 6 g, Saturated Fat: 0.5 g, Trans Fat: 0 g, Cholesterol: 0 mg, Sodium: 502 mg, Potassium: 347 mg

CORN AND BARLEY BAKE

This colorful side dish goes great with saucy pork ribs, chops, or a veggie main dish. It can be made ahead, covered, and refrigerated for up to 2 days. When reheating, stir in an additional ½ cup (125 mL) broth or water.

1 Tbsp (15 mL) canola oil

1 small onion, chopped

1 garlic clove, minced

½ cup (125 mL) chopped sweet red pepper

2 carrots, chopped

1 cup (250 mL) pot or pearl barley

4 cups (1 L) chicken or vegetable broth

2 cups (500 mL) fresh (or frozen and thawed) corn kernels

½ cup (125 mL) chopped fresh parsley

¼ tsp (1 mL) salt

¼ tsp (1 mL) pepper

Preheat oven to 350°F (180°C).

In a large ovenproof saucepan or Dutch oven over medium-high, heat oil. Add onion, garlic, red pepper, and carrots, and sauté for 4 minutes or until onion is softened. Stir in barley, then pour in broth. Cover pan and bake for 1 hour. Stir in corn and parsley; add salt and pepper to taste. Bake for an additional 10 minutes or until heated through and barley is tender.

Makes 8 servings.

Nutritional Information (per serving): Calories: 158, Protein: 5 g, Carbohydrate: 30 g, Fiber: 6 g, Sugars: 4 g, Fat: 3 g, Saturated Fat: 0.4 g, Trans Fat: 0 g, Cholesterol: 0 mg, Sodium: 288 mg, Potassium: 371 mg

BARLEY AND BROCCOLI CASSEROLE

Cut the prep time of this cheese-topped vegetarian side dish by using frozen broccoli and pre-cooking the barley.

½ lb (250 g) broccoli, cut into bite-sized pieces (about 2 cups [500 mL])

1 cup (250 mL) chopped celery

2 cups (500 mL) cooked pot or pearl barley (see Barley Bit)

1 can (10 oz [284 mL]) condensed cream of mushroom soup, undiluted

¾ cup (175 mL) grated cheddar cheese

Preheat oven to 350°F (180°C). Grease an 8-cup (2 L) casserole dish and set aside until needed.

In a medium saucepan of boiling water, cook the broccoli and celery for about 5 minutes or until tender-crisp. Drain, saving ½ cup (125 mL) of the cooking liquid. Arrange the cooked barley in the casserole dish. Top with cooked broccoli and celery. Combine the soup and reserved cooking liquid, then pour over the broccoli. Sprinkle with cheese. Bake uncovered for 35 minutes or until bubbly.

Makes 6 servings.

Nutritional Information (per serving): Calories: 177, Protein: 6 g, Carbohydrate: 22 g, Fiber: 4 g, Sugars: 2 g, Fat: 7 g, Saturated Fat: 3.5 g, Trans Fat: 0 g, Cholesterol: 17 mg, Sodium: 464 mg, Potassium: 250 mg

Barley Bit: Use frozen cooked barley prepared by following the directions on page 6. Thaw before adding it to the casserole. Or in a medium saucepan over high heat, bring 2 cups (500 mL) water or broth to a boil. Stir in 1 cup (250 mL) pot or pearl barley; reduce heat and simmer for 45 minutes.

QUICK AND EASY THREE-GRAIN PILAF Ⓥ

Jazz up an everyday meal with this simple combination of three grains, which works well as a side to fish or roast beef or pork, or as part of a meat-free main course.

⅓ cup (75 mL) pot or pearl barley

⅓ cup (75 mL) wild rice

2 cups (500 mL) beef, chicken, or vegetable broth, divided

⅓ cup (75 mL) brown rice

¼ tsp (1 mL) pepper

In a medium saucepan over high heat, combine the barley and wild rice with 1 cup (250 mL) of the broth; bring to a boil. Cover pan, reduce heat, and simmer for 25 minutes. Add the brown rice and the remaining 1 cup (250 mL) of broth. Continue to simmer for 25 minutes, adding additional broth or water if necessary. Season to taste with pepper.

Makes 6 servings.

Nutritional Information (per serving): Calories: 114, Protein: 4 g, Carbohydrate: 23 g, Fiber: 3 g, Sugars: 0 g, Fat: 0.5 g, Saturated Fat: 0.1 g, Trans Fat: 0 g, Cholesterol: 0 mg, Sodium: 299 mg, Potassium: 93 mg

SAVORY BUTTERNUT SQUASH BARLEY PILAF

Butternut squash has never tasted as good as it does when simmered with barley and herbs in this colorful side dish, which goes great with turkey, chicken, or pork. Briefly blanching the squash makes it easier to peel and cut into pieces.

1 Tbsp (15 mL) olive oil

1 small butternut squash, peeled, seeded, and cut into 1½-inch (4 cm) pieces

1 small yellow onion, chopped

1 small sweet red pepper, chopped

1 cup (250 mL) pot or pearl barley

1 can (10 oz [284 mL]) condensed less-sodium chicken broth, undiluted

1⅔ cup (400 mL) water

½ tsp (2 mL) dried summer savory

½ tsp (2 mL) dried thyme

Salt and freshly ground black pepper, to taste

1 tsp (5 mL) grated lemon rind

In a large pot or Dutch oven over medium-high, heat oil. Add squash, onion, and red pepper, and sauté for 3 minutes. Add barley and sauté for 3 more minutes. Add broth, water, savory, thyme, and salt and pepper to taste. Bring to a boil. Reduce heat, cover pan, and simmer for 30 minutes or until barley is tender, stirring once halfway through. Stir in lemon rind and serve.

Makes 8 servings.

Nutritional Information (per serving): Calories: 137, Protein: 4 g, Carbohydrate: 27 g, Fiber: 5 g, Sugars: 2 g, Fat: 2 g, Saturated Fat: 0.4 g, Trans Fat: 0 g, Cholesterol: 0 mg, Sodium: 100 mg, Potassium: 289 mg

LEMON PARMESAN BARLEY

Looking for a tasty, easy-to-make side dish? This goes great with chicken, fish, or vegetarian dishes. It pairs especially well with the Seafood Kebabs on page 115.

2 Tbsp (30 mL) canola oil

1 shallot, chopped

½ cup (125 mL) pot or pearl barley

1¾ cups (425 mL) water

¼ cup (60 mL) grated Parmesan cheese

1 Tbsp (15 mL) grated lemon rind

2 Tbsp (30 mL) chopped parsley

¼ tsp (1 mL) salt

¼ tsp (1 mL) pepper

In a medium saucepan over medium-high, heat oil. Add shallot and cook, stirring occasionally, until softened, about 2 minutes. Stir in barley and add water. Bring to a boil; reduce heat and cover pan. Simmer for 45 to 50 minutes or until barley is tender. Stir in Parmesan cheese, lemon rind, parsley, salt, and pepper.

Makes 4 servings.

Nutritional Information (per serving): Calories: 176, Protein: 5 g, Carbohydrate: 21 g, Fiber: 4 g, Sugars: 1 g, Fat: 9 g, Saturated Fat: 1.5 g, Trans Fat: 0 g, Cholesterol: 4 mg, Sodium: 230 mg, Potassium: 92 mg

SQUASH, PEAR, AND CRANBERRY SIDE

This barley, squash, and fruit dish is a pleasing accompaniment to pork chops, pork tenderloin, or roast chicken. Briefly blanching the squash makes it easier to peel and dice.

1 large acorn squash

1 Tbsp (15 mL) canola oil

1 small onion, thinly sliced

1 cup (250 mL) pot or pearl barley

1 can (10 oz [284 mL]) condensed less-sodium chicken or vegetable broth, undiluted

2 cups (500 mL) water

2 pears, peeled and diced

¼ cup (60 mL) dried cranberries

2 Tbsp (30 mL) maple syrup or honey

¼ tsp (1 mL) salt

¼ tsp (1 mL) pepper

Microwave squash on high or simmer in boiling water for 1 minute. Cut in half; remove seeds and membranes; peel and dice.

In a large pot or Dutch oven over medium-high, heat oil. Add onion and cook for 1 to 2 minutes. Add squash. Stir and cook for 2 minutes. Stir in barley. Add broth and water; bring to a boil. Cover pan, reduce heat, and simmer for 45 to 50 minutes or until barley is tender. Stir in pears, cranberries, maple syrup or honey, salt, and pepper. Simmer for 5 minutes or until pears are tender.

Makes 8 servings.

Nutritional Information (per serving): Calories: 185, Protein: 4 g, Carbohydrate: 39 g, Fiber: 6 g, Sugars: 11 g, Fat: 2 g, Saturated Fat: 0.3 g, Trans Fat: 0 g, Cholesterol: 4 mg, Sodium: 100 mg, Potassium: 336 mg

SIDES

COCONUT BARLEY

This barley side dish is delicious served with skewers of grilled shrimp or with stir-fried pork.

1 Tbsp (15 mL) canola oil

¼ cup (60 mL) chopped green onion

1 Tbsp (15 mL) minced garlic

2 tsp (10 mL) minced fresh ginger

1 cup (250 mL) pot or pearl barley

2½ cups (625 mL) water

1 cup (250 mL) low-fat coconut milk (see Barley Bit)

¼ tsp (1 mL) salt

Chopped fresh cilantro, for garnish (optional)

In a medium saucepan over medium, heat oil and stir in green onion, garlic, and ginger. Stir and cook for 2 minutes. Stir in barley, water, and coconut milk. Bring to a boil, then reduce heat. Cover pan and simmer for 45 to 55 minutes or until barley is tender, stirring occasionally. Stir in salt. Serve garnished with cilantro, if desired.

Makes 6 servings.

Nutritional Information (per serving): Calories: 185, Protein: 4 g, Carbohydrate: 28 g, Fiber: 5 g, Sugars: 1 g, Fat: 6 g, Saturated Fat: 3 g, Trans Fat: 0 g, Cholesterol: 0 mg, Sodium: 117 mg, Potassium: 109 mg

Barley Bit: The coconut milk may have separated in the container, so give it a good stir before using.

CARROT, PARMESAN, AND BARLEY RISOTTO

Carrots, red onion, and Parmesan cheese combine with barley in this creamy risotto side dish. Substitute a vegetable broth for the chicken broth to make this a vegetarian risotto.

1 Tbsp (15 mL) canola oil

1 small red onion, chopped

6 medium carrots, grated

1 cup (250 mL) pot or pearl barley

1 carton (32 oz [900 mL]) less-sodium, ready-to-use chicken broth

½ cup (125 mL) grated Parmesan cheese

1 Tbsp (15 mL) butter or margarine

¼ tsp (1 mL) salt

¼ tsp (1 mL) pepper

In a large saucepan over medium-high, heat oil. Add onion and carrots and cook, stirring occasionally, until softened, 5 to 7 minutes. Stir in barley. Add chicken broth and bring to a boil. Reduce heat; cover pan and simmer for 55 minutes or until barley is creamy. Remove from heat. Stir in Parmesan cheese, butter or margarine, salt, and pepper.

Makes 4 servings.

Nutritional Information (per serving): Calories: 344, Protein: 14 g, Carbohydrate: 51 g, Fiber: 11 g, Sugars: 7 g, Fat: 11 g, Saturated Fat: 4.5 g, Trans Fat: 0.1 g, Cholesterol: 21 mg, Sodium: 527 mg, Potassium: 476 mg

BAKING

BARLEY BANANA BREAD

This healthy version of classic banana bread has the added fiber of barley flour. Applesauce replaces some of the fat normally used in the moist bread.

1 cup (250 mL) whole barley flour

½ cup (125 mL) all-purpose flour

1 cup (250 mL) granulated sugar

2 tsp (10 mL) baking powder

1 tsp (5 mL) baking soda

⅓ cup (75 mL) canola oil

¼ cup (60 mL) sweetened applesauce

1 tsp (5 mL) vanilla

3 ripe medium bananas, mashed (1½ cups [375 mL])

Preheat oven to 350°F (180°C). Lightly spray a 9 × 5 inch (23 × 13 cm) loaf pan with non-stick cooking spray or line with parchment paper.

In a medium bowl, combine barley flour, all-purpose flour, sugar, baking powder, and baking soda. In another bowl, combine canola oil, applesauce, vanilla, and bananas. Add to dry ingredients, stirring until mixture is lumpy but just blended. Pour batter into pan. Bake for 50 to 55 minutes or until loaf is golden brown on top and a cake tester or toothpick inserted in the center comes out clean. Cool for 10 minutes. Then turn loaf out of pan and cool on a rack.

Makes 1 loaf (about 16 slices).

Nutritional Information (per slice): Calories: 151, Protein: 1 g, Carbohydrate: 27 g, Fiber: 2 g, Sugars: 17 g, Fat: 6 g, Saturated Fat: 0.3 g, Trans Fat: 0 g, Cholesterol: 0 mg, Sodium: 124 mg, Potassium: 8 mg

CRANBERRY ORANGE LOAF

The addition of barley flour adds a nutty flavor and rustic look to this cranberry tea bread. Serve with tea or coffee or, as a breakfast treat, spread with cream cheese.

1 cup (250 mL) whole barley flour

1 cup (250 mL) all-purpose flour

¾ cup (175 mL) granulated sugar

2 tsp (10 mL) baking powder

1 tsp (5 mL) salt

½ tsp (2 mL) baking soda

¼ cup (60 mL) butter or margarine

2 eggs, beaten

¾ cup (175 mL) orange juice

1 Tbsp (15 mL) orange rind

1 cup (250 mL) fresh (or frozen and thawed) cranberries, chopped

⅓ cup (75 mL) pecans, chopped

Preheat oven to 350°F (180°C). Lightly spray a 9 × 5 inch (23 × 13 cm) loaf pan with non-stick cooking spray or line with parchment paper.

In a large bowl, combine barley flour, all-purpose flour, sugar, baking powder, salt, and baking soda. Cut in butter until mixture resembles coarse cornmeal. In another bowl, combine eggs, orange juice, and orange rind; pour over dry ingredients and mix until dry ingredients are just blended. Fold cranberries and nuts into batter. Pour batter into pan. Bake for 55 to 60 minutes or until a cake tester or toothpick inserted in the center comes out clean. Cool for 10 minutes. Then turn loaf out of pan and cool on rack.

Makes 1 loaf (16 slices).

Nutritional Information (per slice): Calories: 146, Protein: 2 g, Carbohydrate: 23 g, Fiber: 2 g, Sugars: 11 g, Fat: 6 g, Saturated Fat: 2 g, Trans Fat: 0.1 g, Cholesterol: 32 mg, Sodium: 266 mg, Potassium: 55 mg

POPPY SEED LEMON LOAF

(V)

This lemon loaf is flecked with poppy seeds and flavored with nutty barley flour. While still warm from the oven, brush with a glaze of icing sugar and lemon juice.

Loaf

1 cup (250 mL) whole barley flour

1 cup (250 mL) all-purpose flour

1 cup (250 mL) granulated sugar

2 tsp (10 mL) baking powder

1 tsp (5 mL) ground nutmeg

½ tsp (2 mL) ground ginger

¼ tsp (1 mL) salt

¼ cup (60 mL) poppy seeds

1 egg

¾ cup (175 mL) buttermilk

½ cup (125 mL) canola oil

2 Tbsp (30 mL) grated lemon rind

Glaze

⅓ cup (75 mL) icing sugar

1 Tbsp (15 mL) lemon juice

Preheat oven to 350°F (180°C). Lightly grease a 9 × 5 inch (23 × 13 cm) loaf pan.

In a medium bowl, mix together barley flour, all-purpose flour, sugar, baking powder, nutmeg, ginger, and salt. Stir in poppy seeds. In another medium bowl, beat egg, buttermilk, oil, and lemon rind. Stir the flour mixture into the liquid mixture until well blended. Pour batter into pan and bake for 50 to 55 minutes or until a cake tester or toothpick inserted in the center comes out clean. Place pan on wire rack to cool loaf for 5 minutes.

Meanwhile, in a small bowl, combine icing sugar and lemon juice. Turn bread out of pan onto rack and brush top with glaze.

Makes 1 loaf (16 slices).

Nutritional Information (per slice, with glaze): Calories: 200, Protein: 3 g, Carbohydrate: 28 g, Fiber: 2 g, Sugars: 16 g, Fat: 9 g, Saturated Fat: 1 g, Trans Fat: 0 g, Cholesterol: 13 mg, Sodium: 99 mg, Potassium: 32 mg

CHOCOLATE GINGER LOAF

This unusual chocolate loaf is made with barley flour plus dark baking chocolate, mascarpone cheese, and crystallized ginger.

1½ cups (375 mL) all-purpose flour

¾ cup (175 mL) whole barley flour

1 tsp (5 mL) baking powder

¼ tsp (1 mL) salt

4 oz (112 g) (4 squares) 70% dark chocolate, coarsely chopped

¾ cup (175 mL) mascarpone cheese

½ cup (125 mL) unsalted butter, softened

1 cup (250 mL) granulated sugar

4 eggs

1 tsp (5 mL) vanilla

½ cup (125 mL) diced crystallized ginger

Preheat oven to 350°F (180°C). Lightly grease a 9 × 5 inch (23 × 13 cm) loaf pan.

In a medium bowl, combine all-purpose flour, barley flour, baking powder, and salt. In a medium saucepan over low heat, melt chocolate. Add cheese to warm chocolate and stir until combined. In a large bowl, beat butter until creamy. Gradually beat in sugar. Add eggs, one at a time, beating well after each addition. Beat in vanilla. Gradually beat in flour mixture, then stir in chocolate mixture and ginger. Turn batter into pan and bake until a cake tester or toothpick inserted into the center comes out clean, 65 to 75 minutes. Cover top loosely with foil if edges or center of loaf become too brown. Remove from oven and cool in pan for 15 minutes before turning out onto rack.

Makes 1 loaf (12 slices).

Nutritional Information (per slice, without glaze): Calories: 430, Protein: 7 g, Carbohydrate: 46 g, Fiber: 2 g, Sugars: 24 g, Fat: 25 g, Saturated Fat: 15 g, Trans Fat: 0.2 g, Cholesterol: 120 mg, Sodium: 131 mg, Potassium: 40 mg

Barley Bit: To make this loaf even more of a standout, when completely cool, drizzle with 1¼ cups (310 mL) sifted icing sugar mixed with 3 tablespoons (45 mL) water and ¼ teaspoon (1 mL) vanilla. Then sprinkle with chopped toasted almonds.

HERBED COTTAGE CHEESE PAN BREAD

This simple twist on the classic cottage cheese bread uses barley flour as well as all-purpose flour and is flavored with a mixture of dried herbs.

1½ cups (375 mL) whole barley flour

½ cup (125 mL) all-purpose flour

1 Tbsp (15 mL) baking powder

1 tsp (5 mL) salt

1 tsp (5 mL) mixed dried herbs (oregano, thyme, basil, rosemary)

1 container (8 oz [250 g]) 2% cottage cheese

⅓ cup (75 mL) canola oil

3 Tbsp (45 mL) milk

Preheat oven to 400°F (200°C). Grease a baking sheet.

In a medium bowl, combine barley flour, all-purpose flour, baking powder, salt, and herbs. In a food processor or blender, process cottage cheese, oil, and milk until smooth, then add to flour mixture, stirring just until dry ingredients are moistened.

With lightly floured hands, shape dough into a ball. Place on the baking sheet and gently pat into a ¾-inch (2 cm) thick circle. With a floured knife, cut circle into 10 wedges; separate each wedge slightly and bake for 25 to 30 minutes until browned and a cake tester or toothpick inserted in the center of a wedge comes out clean.

Makes 10 wedges.

Nutritional Information (per wedge): Calories: 167, Protein: 4 g, Carbohydrate: 18 g, Fiber: 2 g, Sugars: 2 g, Fat: 11 g, Saturated Fat: 1 g, Trans Fat: 0 g, Cholesterol: 3 mg, Sodium: 430 mg, Potassium: 36 mg

BEST BARLEY BREAD

Barley flour adds a wonderful nutty flavor to this bread. It's mixed with white flour to ensure the bread rises properly. Knead the dough in one direction to develop long strands of gluten, which make the dough rise evenly.

3¾ cups (925 mL) warm water

3 Tbsp (45 mL) honey or sugar

3 envelopes (¼ oz [8 g] each) regular dry yeast (2 Tbsp plus ¾ tsp [34 mL])

2¼ cups (560 mL) whole barley flour

1 Tbsp (15 mL) salt

6¾ cups (1.675 L) all-purpose flour, divided

3 Tbsp (45 mL) lemon juice

3 Tbsp (45 mL) canola oil

Measure water and check temperature so that it is between 100°F and 110°F (38°C and 43°C). Pour water into a large mixing bowl and combine with honey or sugar and yeast. Let rest for about 10 minutes to proof the yeast. Stir the barley flour, salt, and 2 cups (500 mL) of the all-purpose flour into the yeast mixture. Add the lemon juice and oil, then slowly add the remaining flour. When the mixture becomes quite difficult to handle, turn it out of the bowl onto a lightly floured surface and knead vigorously for 10 minutes, or knead for 5 minutes in a bread machine, adding more all-purpose flour if necessary. Cover the dough with a damp cloth and let it rest for 20 minutes.

Grease three 9 × 5 inch (23 × 13 cm) loaf pans. Once dough is rested, knead by hand again for 2 to 3 minutes. Form into 3 loaves and put in pans. Cover each with a damp cloth and let rise until dough doubles in bulk, about 1 hour.

Preheat oven to 375°F (190°C). Bake loaves for 25 to 30 minutes or until golden brown and the bread sounds hollow when tapped. Immediately turn out onto racks to cool.

Makes 3 loaves (about 18 slices each).

Nutritional Information (per slice): Calories: 126, Protein: 3 g, Carbohydrate: 25 g, Fiber: 2 g, Sugars: 2 g, Fat: 2.5 g, Saturated Fat: 0.1 g, Trans Fat: 0.1 g, Cholesterol: 0 mg, Sodium: 198 mg, Potassium: 33 mg

APRICOT HONEY BARLEY BREAD MADE IN A BREAD MACHINE

Barley flour can be successfully used in bread machines, as evidenced by this sweet fruited bread, which makes wonderful toast. This recipe can also be used to make a more basic honey barley bread. Just omit the apricots, sunflower seeds, and cinnamon.

1⅓ cups (325 mL) warm water

2 Tbsp (30 mL) canola oil

3 Tbsp (45 mL) honey

1 Tbsp (15 mL) lemon juice

1½ tsp (7 mL) salt

3 cups (750 mL) all-purpose flour or bread flour

1 cup (250 mL) whole barley flour

⅓ cup (75 mL) chopped dried apricots

2 Tbsp (30 mL) raw sunflower seeds

1½ tsp (7 mL) ground cinnamon

2 tsp (10 mL) bread machine yeast

Add all ingredients to the bread machine pan in the order listed, or as recommended by the instructions for your bread machine. Insert the pan into the oven chamber. Select basic bread cycle and start machine as directed.

Makes 1 loaf (18 slices).

Nutritional Information (per slice): Calories: 136, Protein: 3 g, Carbohydrate: 26 g, Fiber: 2 g, Sugars: 3 g, Fat: 2 g, Saturated Fat: 0.2 g, Trans Fat: 0 g, Cholesterol: 0 mg, Sodium: 199 mg, Potassium: 30 mg

BREAD MACHINE CARROT POPPY SEED LOAF

This yeast bread includes unusual ingredients like carrots, poppy seeds, and barley flour. It is an unexpected but delicious treat!

1 cup (250 mL) warm water

¾ cup (175 mL) finely shredded carrot, lightly packed

2 Tbsp (30 mL) canola oil

1 tsp (5 mL) salt

3 cups (750 mL) all-purpose flour

1 cup (250 mL) whole barley flour

1 Tbsp (15 mL) packed brown sugar

3 Tbsp (45 mL) poppy seeds

2 tsp (10 mL) bread machine yeast

Add all ingredients to the bread machine pan in the order listed, or as recommended by the instructions for your bread machine. Insert the pan into the oven chamber. Select basic bread cycle and start machine as directed.

Makes 1 loaf (16 slices).

Nutritional Information (per slice): Calories: 145, Protein: 4 g, Carbohydrate: 26 g, Fiber: 2 g, Sugars: 1 g, Fat: 3 g, Saturated Fat: 0.3 g, Trans Fat: 0 g, Cholesterol: 0 mg, Sodium: 153 mg, Potassium: 49 mg

RASPBERRY BANANA MUFFINS

Raspberries and ripe bananas paired with nutty-flavored barley flour make these muffins extra special. If fresh raspberries are not available, use frozen.

1 cup (250 mL) whole barley flour

1 cup (250 mL) all-purpose flour

¾ cup (175 mL) granulated sugar

2 tsp (10 mL) baking powder

½ tsp (2 mL) salt

2 eggs

¼ cup (60 mL) milk

¼ cup (60 mL) canola oil

2 ripe medium bananas, mashed (1 cup [250 mL])

¾ cup (175 mL) fresh or frozen unsweetened raspberries (see Barley Bit)

Preheat oven to 375°F (190°C). Lightly grease a medium 12-cup muffin tray.

In a medium bowl, combine barley flour, all-purpose flour, sugar, baking powder, and salt. In a large bowl, lightly beat eggs. Stir in milk, oil, and bananas. Add flour mixture and stir until just moistened. Stir in raspberries. Spoon batter into muffin cups. Bake for 20 to 25 minutes or until the top of a muffin springs back when lightly touched in the center.

Makes 12 muffins.

Nutritional Information (per muffin): Calories: 194, Protein: 3 g, Carbohydrate: 33 g, Fiber: 2 g, Sugars: 16 g, Fat: 7 g, Saturated Fat: 1 g, Trans Fat: 0 g, Cholesterol: 32 mg, Sodium: 173 mg, Potassium: 111 mg

Barley Bit: If using frozen raspberries, do not thaw. Gently stir raspberries into the batter so they don't break apart.

BLUEBERRY BARLEY MUFFINS

V

You'll notice the wonderful texture and flavor in these blueberry muffins made with barley flour. The recipe works equally well with fresh or frozen blueberries.

2 cups (500 mL) whole barley flour

½ cup (125 mL) granulated sugar

4 tsp (20 mL) baking powder

½ tsp (2 mL) salt

½ tsp (2 mL) ground cinnamon

1 cup (250 mL) fresh or frozen blueberries (see Barley Bit)

2 eggs

1 cup (250 mL) milk

¼ cup (60 mL) canola oil

Preheat oven to 400°F (200°C). Lightly grease a medium 12-cup muffin tray, or line the cups with paper liners.

In a large bowl, combine barley flour, sugar, baking powder, salt, cinnamon, and blueberries. In a small bowl, lightly beat eggs; stir in milk and oil and pour into the flour mixture. Stir until just combined. Spoon batter into each muffin cup until almost full. Bake for 18 minutes or until the top of a muffin springs back when lightly touched in the center.

Makes 12 muffins.

Nutritional Information (per muffin): Calories: 164, Protein: 2 g, Carbohydrate: 25 g, Fiber: 3 g, Sugars: 11 g, Fat: 9 g, Saturated Fat: 0.5 g, Trans Fat: 0 g, Cholesterol: 33 mg, Sodium: 240 mg, Potassium: 51 mg

Barley Bit: If using frozen blueberries, do not thaw. Gently stir blueberries into the batter so they don't discolor the muffins.

RHUBARB PECAN MUFFINS

These tangy wholesome muffins get rave reviews whenever they are served. Fresh or frozen rhubarb can be used or, if you wish, substitute with chopped fresh or frozen cranberries. The streusel topping is optional.

Muffins

1 cup (250 mL) whole barley flour

1 cup (250 mL) all-purpose flour

¾ cup (175 mL) granulated sugar

1½ tsp (7 mL) baking powder

½ tsp (2 mL) baking soda

1 tsp (5 mL) salt

1 egg

¼ cup (60 mL) canola oil

2 tsp (10 mL) grated orange peel

¾ cup (175 mL) orange juice

1½ cups (375 mL) finely chopped rhubarb

¾ cup (175 mL) chopped pecans

Streusel Topping (optional)

½ cup (125 mL) quick-cooking rolled oats

½ cup (125 mL) brown sugar

¼ cup (60 mL) chopped pecans

¼ tsp (1 mL) ground cinnamon

¼ tsp (1 mL) ground ginger

¼ cup (60 mL) melted butter

Preheat oven to 375°F (190°C). Lightly grease a medium 12-cup muffin tray, or spray pan with non-stick cooking spray.

In a large bowl, combine barley flour, all-purpose flour, sugar, baking powder, baking soda, and salt. In another bowl, combine egg, canola oil, orange peel, and orange juice. Add to dry ingredients along with rhubarb and pecans. Spoon into prepared pan.

If using topping, combine all ingredients in a small bowl. Sprinkle 1 tablespoon (15 mL) of the topping onto each muffin.

Bake muffins for 25 minutes or until tops are firm to the touch.

Makes 12 muffins.

Nutritional Information (per muffin): No Topping (With Topping), Calories: 223 (322), Protein: 2 g (3 g), Carbohydrate: 31 g (43 g), Fiber: 2 g (3 g), Sugars: 15 g (24 g), Fat: 12 g (17 g), Saturated Fat: 1 g (3.5 g), Trans Fat: 0 g (0.2 g), Cholesterol: 16 mg (26 mg), Sodium: 301 mg (338 mg), Potassium: 120 mg (143 mg)

CHOCOLATE BANANA MUFFINS

The secret to good muffins is to not over-mix them. So when stirring the liquid ingredients into the dry ingredients, stir until they are just barely combined.

1 cup (250 mL) whole barley flour

1 cup (250 mL) all-purpose flour

¼ cup (60 mL) packed brown sugar

¼ cup (60 mL) unsweetened cocoa powder

2 tsp (10 mL) baking powder

1 tsp (5 mL) baking soda

¼ tsp (1 mL) salt

¼ tsp (1 mL) ground cinnamon

¼ tsp (1 mL) ground nutmeg

2 eggs

½ cup (125 mL) milk

3 Tbsp (45 mL) canola oil

2 ripe medium bananas, mashed (1 cup [250 mL])

⅓ cup (75 mL) maple syrup

1 tsp (5 mL) vanilla

Preheat oven to 400°F (200°C). Lightly grease a medium 12-cup muffin tray, or line cups with paper liners.

In a large bowl, combine barley flour, all-purpose flour, brown sugar, cocoa powder, baking powder, baking soda, salt, cinnamon, and nutmeg. In a medium bowl, lightly beat eggs. Stir in milk, oil, bananas, maple syrup, and vanilla, then pour into flour mixture. Stir until just combined. Spoon into muffin cups. Bake for 20 minutes or until the top of a muffin springs back when lightly touched in the center.

Makes 12 muffins.

Nutritional Information (per muffin): Calories: 180, Protein: 3 g, Carbohydrate: 32 g, Fiber: 3 g, Sugars: 13 g, Fat: 6 g, Saturated Fat: 1 g, Trans Fat: 0 g, Cholesterol: 33 mg, Sodium: 233 mg, Potassium: 160 mg

ORANGE, DATE, AND PECAN BRAN MUFFINS

Chopped dates, pecans, and orange rind are added to these rustic bran muffins made with barley flour. Garnished with half a date, one of these muffins makes a nutritious snack or treat with a salad at lunch.

1 cup (250 mL) wheat bran

¾ cup (175 mL) whole barley flour

¾ cup (175 mL) all-purpose flour

⅓ cup (75 mL) packed brown sugar

1½ tsp (7 mL) baking powder

½ tsp (2 mL) baking soda

Grated rind from 1 medium orange

¾ cup (175 mL) chopped dates

½ cup (125 mL) chopped pecans

1 egg

1 cup (250 mL) buttermilk

¼ cup (60 mL) canola oil

¼ cup (60 mL) molasses

Preheat oven to 375°F (190°C). Lightly grease a 12-cup muffin tray.

In a large bowl, stir together bran, barley flour, all-purpose flour, brown sugar, baking powder, baking soda, and orange rind. Add dates and pecans. In a small bowl, beat egg; stir in buttermilk, oil, and molasses. Pour liquid mixture over dry ingredients and stir just until moistened. Spoon batter into muffin cups. Bake for 20 to 25 minutes or until tops are firm to the touch. Cool on a wire rack.

Makes 12 muffins.

Nutritional Information (per muffin): Calories: 222, Protein: 3 g, Carbohydrate: 35 g, Fiber: 4 g, Sugars: 18 g, Fat: 10 g, Saturated Fat: 1 g, Trans Fat: 0 g, Cholesterol: 17 mg, Sodium: 128 mg, Potassium: 233 mg

CHEESE, ONION, AND BACON SCONES

These savory golden scones are delicious for breakfast or brunch. They would also make an excellent accompaniment to a lunch or supper salad.

2 cups (500 mL) whole barley flour

1 tsp (5 mL) baking powder

1 tsp (5 mL) powdered mustard

½ tsp (2 mL) salt

½ cup (125 mL) unsalted butter, cut into chunks

1 cup (250 mL) shredded old cheddar cheese

½ cup (125 mL) cooked bacon bits

¼ cup (60 mL) chopped green onion

¾ cup (175 mL) milk

Preheat oven to 400°F (200°C). Lightly grease a baking sheet.

In a large bowl, combine flour, baking powder, powdered mustard, and salt. Cut in butter until mixture resembles coarse crumbs. Stir in cheese, bacon, and green onion. Add milk and stir until dry ingredients are moistened. With lightly floured hands, transfer dough to a lightly floured surface and knead several times. Place dough on the baking sheet and flatten into a round about 1-inch (2.5 cm) thick. Cut with a knife into 8 triangles and separate slightly. Bake until scones are golden, 20 to 25 minutes.

Makes 8 scones.

Nutritional Information (per scone): Calories: 298, Protein: 8 g, Carbohydrate: 22 g, Fiber: 4 g, Sugars: 2 g, Fat: 23 g, Saturated Fat: 11 g, Trans Fat: 0.4 g, Cholesterol: 54 mg, Sodium: 465 mg, Potassium: 46 mg

CHOCOLATE CHUNK CHERRY CREAM SCONES

Indulge your love for chocolate and cherries with these decadent scones. When served slightly warm, the chunks of dark chocolate are still slightly gooey.

2 cups (500 mL) whole barley flour

1 cup (250 mL) all-purpose flour

¼ cup (60 mL) granulated sugar

1 Tbsp (15 mL) baking powder

¼ tsp (1 mL) salt

½ cup (125 mL) cold butter

¾ cup (175 mL) light cream

1 egg

2½ oz (70 g) (2½ squares) 70% dark chocolate, cut into chunks (about ½ cup [125 mL])

½ cup (125 mL) dried cherries

½ cup (125 mL) chopped pecans

Preheat oven to 350°F (180°C). Lightly grease a baking sheet or line it with parchment paper.

In a large bowl, mix barley flour, all-purpose flour, sugar, baking powder, and salt. Cut butter into flour mixture until it resembles coarse crumbs. In a small bowl, whisk together cream and egg. Reserve 2 tablespoons (30 mL) of the egg mixture and add remainder to the flour mixture along with the chocolate, cherries, and pecans. Stir with a fork just until evenly moistened. With lightly floured hands, gather dough into a ball and place on baking sheet. Flatten into a round about 1¾ inches (4.5 cm) thick. Cut into 8 wedges. Separate the wedges slightly and brush with reserved egg mixture. Bake scones until tops are brown, 25 to 30 minutes. Serve warm or cold.

Makes 8 scones.

Nutritional Information (per scone): Calories: 484, Protein: 5 g, Carbohydrate: 51 g, Fiber: 6 g, Sugars: 14 g, Fat: 32 g, Saturated Fat: 15 g, Trans Fat: 0.5 g, Cholesterol: 80 mg, Sodium: 329 mg, Potassium: 145 mg

YOGURT BARLEY FRUIT SCONES

Fresh-baked scones are a comfort food equally relished at breakfast or with a mid-afternoon cup of tea. These barley scones are made with extra thick (Greek-style) yogurt and raisins or dried cranberries.

2 cups (500 mL) whole barley flour

2 Tbsp (30 mL) granulated sugar

2½ tsp (12 mL) baking powder

½ tsp (2 mL) baking soda

1 egg

1 cup (250 mL) extra thick (Greek-style) plain yogurt

1 Tbsp (15 mL) canola oil

½ cup (125 mL) raisins, currants, or dried cranberries

Preheat oven to 375°F (190°C). Lightly grease a baking sheet.

In a large bowl, mix together barley flour, sugar, baking powder, and baking soda. In a separate bowl, lightly beat egg and combine with yogurt and oil; stir into flour mixture, along with dried fruit. With lightly floured hands, gather dough into a ball and place it on the baking sheet. Flatten into a round about ¾-inch (2 cm) thick. Cut with a knife to divide into 6 scones. Spread pieces apart on baking sheet. Bake for 20 to 25 minutes or until lightly browned and a cake tester or toothpick inserted in the center comes out clean. Serve warm.

Makes 6 scones.

Nutritional Information (per scone): With Raisins (With Cranberries), Calories: 243 (230), Protein: 5 g (4 g), Carbohydrate: 43 g (41 g), Fiber: 5 g (5 g), Sugars: 16 g (13 g), Fat: 10 g (10 g), Saturated Fat: 1 g (1 g), Trans Fat: 0 g (0 g), Cholesterol: 35 mg (35 mg), Sodium: 283 mg (280 mg), Potassium: 114 mg (14 m)g

EASY RAISIN CINNAMON SWIRLS

Your guests or children will gobble up these quick swirls fresh and warm from the oven.

Swirls

2 cups (500 mL) whole barley flour

1 cup (250 mL) all-purpose flour

½ cup (125 mL) granulated sugar

1 Tbsp (15 mL) baking powder

½ tsp (2 mL) salt

¾ cup (175 mL) butter or margarine

2 large eggs

½ cup (125 mL) milk

2 Tbsp (30 mL) melted butter or margarine

3 Tbsp (45 mL) packed brown sugar

¼ tsp (1 mL) ground cinnamon

⅓ cup (75 mL) raisins

Glaze

1 cup (250 mL) icing sugar

2 Tbsp (30 mL) milk or water

Preheat oven to 375°F (190°C). Grease a medium 12-cup muffin pan.

In a large bowl, mix barley flour, all-purpose flour, sugar, baking powder, and salt. Cut in butter or margarine until mixture resembles coarse crumbs. In a small bowl, combine eggs and milk, then add to dry ingredients, mixing until a nice dough forms.

On a lightly floured board, press and roll the dough into a 12 × 18 inch (30 × 45 cm) rectangle. Brush with melted butter or margarine and sprinkle with brown sugar, cinnamon, and raisins. Roll up dough into a tube shape and slice into 12 sections. Place 1 slice into each muffin cup. Bake for 15 to 20 minutes or until golden. Allow to cool slightly.

In a small bowl, mix icing sugar with milk or water to make a smooth, runny glaze. Drizzle each swirl with glaze when still warm.

Makes 12 swirls.

Nutritional Information (per swirl, with icing): Calories: 334, Protein: 3 g, Carbohydrate: 47 g, Fiber: 3 g, Sugars: 25 g, Fat: 17 g, Saturated Fat: 9 g, Trans Fat: 0.5 g, Cholesterol: 68 mg, Sodium: 326 mg, Potassium: 79 mg

SMART COOKIES

These chunky peanut butter cookies with raisins and chocolate chips go great in a lunchbox. It's not necessary to grease the cookie sheet, because the dough contains enough margarine to prevent the baked cookie from sticking.

¼ cup (60 mL) peanut butter

¼ cup (60 mL) margarine

⅓ cup (75 mL) packed brown sugar

⅓ cup (75 mL) granulated sugar

½ tsp (2 mL) vanilla

1 egg

¾ cup (175 mL) whole barley flour

½ tsp (2 mL) baking soda

½ tsp (2 mL) salt

½ cup (125 mL) quick-cooking rolled oats

½ cup (125 mL) cornflakes

½ cup (125 mL) raisins or nuts

½ cup (125 mL) chocolate chips

1 tsp (5 mL) water

Preheat oven to 375°F (190°C).

In a large bowl, beat together peanut butter, margarine, brown sugar, and granulated sugar until smooth. Beat in vanilla and egg. Add flour, baking soda, and salt. Stir until combined. Mix in oats, cornflakes, raisins or nuts, chocolate chips, and water. Drop dough by heaping teaspoonfuls onto a cookie sheet, 2 inches (5 cm) apart. Bake for 10 to 12 minutes.

Makes about 24 cookies.

Nutritional Information (per cookie): Calories: 107, Protein: 1 g, Carbohydrate: 15 g, Fiber: 1 g, Sugars: 11 g, Fat: 5 g, Saturated Fat: 1.5 g, Trans Fat: 0.3 g, Cholesterol: 8 mg, Sodium: 114 mg, Potassium: 64 mg

APPLESAUCE RAISIN COOKIES

These spicy raisin cookies, made with barley flour and oats, are a family favorite.

¼ cup (60 mL) sweetened applesauce

¼ cup (60 mL) canola oil

½ cup (125 mL) packed brown sugar

1 egg

½ tsp (2 mL) baking soda

½ tsp (2 mL) salt

½ tsp (2 mL) ground cinnamon

¼ tsp (1 mL) ground ginger

¼ tsp (1 mL) ground nutmeg

½ tsp (2 mL) vanilla

1 cup (250 mL) quick-cooking rolled oats

1 cup less 2 Tbsp (220 mL) whole barley flour

½ cup (125 mL) raisins (see Barley Bit)

Preheat oven to 350°F (180°C). Grease a cookie sheet.

In a large bowl, cream together applesauce, oil, and brown sugar. Beat in egg. Add baking soda, salt, cinnamon, ginger, nutmeg, vanilla, oats, barley flour, and raisins. Mix until well combined. Drop dough by heaping teaspoonfuls onto a cookie sheet, 2 inches (5 cm) apart. Bake for 10 to 12 minutes.

Makes about 18 cookies.

Nutritional Information (per cookie): Calories: 108, Protein: 1 g, Carbohydrate: 17 g, Fiber: 1 g, Sugars: 10 g, Fat: 4.5 g, Saturated Fat: 0.3 g, Trans Fat: 0 g, Cholesterol: 11 mg, Sodium: 107 mg, Potassium: 49 mg

Barley Bit: If your raisins are dry and hard, pour boiling water over them and let stand for 5 minutes; drain and pat dry before adding to the dough.

CRISPY BARLEY RAISIN COOKIES

Ⓥ

These well-spiced crisp cookies combine barley flour and barley flakes and are studded with yummy raisins.

1 cup (250 mL) butter or margarine, softened

1 cup (250 mL) packed brown sugar

1 egg

1½ tsp (7 mL) vanilla

1½ cups (375 mL) whole barley flour

1 tsp (5 mL) baking soda

½ tsp (2 mL) salt

1 tsp (5 mL) ground cinnamon

½ tsp (2 mL) ground ginger

¼ tsp (1 mL) ground nutmeg

1½ cups (375 mL) barley flakes or quick-cooking rolled oats

1 cup (250 mL) raisins

Preheat oven to 350°F (180°C). Grease a couple of cookie sheets.

In a large bowl, beat together butter or margarine and brown sugar. Beat in egg and vanilla. In another bowl, combine barley flour, baking soda, salt, cinnamon, ginger, and nutmeg. Stir into creamed mixture. Stir in barley flakes or rolled oats and raisins.

Drop dough by heaping teaspoonfuls onto cookie sheets, 2 inches (5 cm) apart. Bake for 9 to 11 minutes.

Makes about 36 cookies.

Nutritional Information (per cookie): Calories: 115, Protein: 1 g, Carbohydrate: 16 g, Fiber: 1 g, Sugars: 9 g, Fat: 6 g, Saturated Fat: 3 g, Trans Fat: 0.2 g, Cholesterol: 19 mg, Sodium: 118 mg, Potassium: 47 mg

CHOCOLATE AND CHOCOLATE CHIP COOKIES

Here are the cookies to satisfy your chocolate craving. They're made with two chocolate ingredients—unsweetened cocoa powder and chocolate chips.

2 cups (500 mL) whole barley flour

½ cup (125 mL) unsweetened cocoa powder

1 tsp (5 mL) baking soda

½ tsp (2 mL) salt

1 cup (250 mL) butter or margarine, softened

¾ cup (175 mL) granulated sugar

½ cup (125 mL) packed brown sugar

1 tsp (5 mL) vanilla

2 eggs

1⅓ cups (325 mL) semi-sweet chocolate chips

Preheat oven to 350°F (180°C).

In a medium bowl, mix flour, cocoa powder, baking soda, and salt. In a large bowl, cream butter or margarine and gradually add granulated sugar and brown sugar. Beat in vanilla, then beat in eggs. Gradually stir flour mixture into egg mixture. Stir in chocolate chips. Drop dough by rounded tablespoonfuls onto ungreased baking sheets, 2 inches (5 cm) apart. Bake for 9 to 11 minutes or until centers are set but still soft. Cool cookies on baking sheets for 2 minutes and then remove to wire racks to cool completely.

Makes about 36 cookies.

Nutritional Information (per cookie): Calories: 133, Protein: 1 g, Carbohydrate: 16 g, Fiber: 1 g, Sugars: 11 g, Fat: 8 g, Saturated Fat: 4.5 g, Trans Fat: 0.2 g, Cholesterol: 24 mg, Sodium: 118 mg, Potassium: 32 mg

OLDE FASHIONED GINGERSNAPS

Barley flour makes melt-in-your-mouth gingersnaps. These have just the right blend of ginger and cinnamon, and the dough is easy to handle. Store the baked cookies in an airtight container to keep them crisp.

2¼ cups (560 mL) whole barley flour

2 tsp (10 mL) baking soda

2 tsp (10 mL) ground ginger

1 tsp (5 mL) ground cinnamon

½ tsp (2 mL) salt

¾ cup (175 mL) butter or margarine, softened

1¼ cup (310 mL) granulated sugar, divided

1 egg

¼ cup (60 mL) molasses

Preheat oven to 350°F (180°C).

In a medium bowl, combine flour, baking soda, ginger, cinnamon, and salt. In a large bowl, beat butter or margarine until creamy. Gradually beat in 1 cup (250 mL) of the sugar. Place remaining ¼ cup (60 mL) of sugar in a small bowl. Beat egg and molasses into butter mixture. Gradually stir in flour mixture and continue mixing until a soft dough forms. Shape dough into 1-inch (2.5 cm) balls and roll each ball in remaining sugar until coated. Place balls 2 inches (5 cm) apart on an ungreased baking sheet. Bake for 10 to 12 minutes or until tops are rounded and slightly cracked. Remove from oven and let set for 3 minutes, then remove to wire racks to cool.

Makes about 48 cookies.

Nutritional Information (per cookie): Calories: 70, Protein: 0.2 g, Carbohydrate: 10 g, Fiber: 1 g, Sugars: 6 g, Fat: 4 g, Saturated Fat: 2 g, Trans Fat: 0.1 g, Cholesterol: 12 mg, Sodium: 104 mg, Potassium: 28 mg

SPICED AND ICED PECAN COCONUT COOKIES

These wholesome spiced drop cookies are made with barley flour and oats, decorated with almond icing, and sprinkled with pecans and coconut. If you manage to squirrel some away, they freeze well and add a fancy touch to a plate of assorted cookies.

1 cup (250 mL) butter or margarine, softened

1¼ cups (310 mL) packed brown sugar

¾ cup (175 mL) granulated sugar

2 eggs

3 tsp (15 mL) vanilla, divided

2 cups (500 mL) whole barley flour

1½ tsp (7 mL) baking soda

¾ tsp (4 mL) salt

3 cups (750 mL) quick-cooking rolled oats or barley flakes

1 tsp (5 mL) ground nutmeg

½ tsp (2 mL) ground cinnamon

3 cups (750 mL) icing sugar

½ tsp (2 mL) almond flavoring

¼ cup (60 mL) light cream

½ cup (125 mL) finely chopped pecans

½ cup (125 mL) fine coconut

Preheat oven to 375°F (190°C).

In a large bowl, cream butter, then beat in brown sugar and granulated sugar. Stir in eggs and 2 teaspoons (10 mL) of the vanilla. In a separate bowl, combine barley flour, baking soda, salt, rolled oats or barley flakes, nutmeg, and cinnamon; stir into creamed butter until dry ingredients are moistened. Drop by teaspoonfuls 2 inches (5 cm) apart onto ungreased cookie sheets. Bake until lightly browned, about 10 minutes. Cool on pan for 10 minutes, then remove to cooling racks.

Place icing sugar in a medium bowl. Mix together remaining 1 teaspoon (5 mL) of vanilla, almond flavoring, and cream, then stir into icing sugar until smooth. Spread icing over cooled cookies and then sprinkle with pecans and coconut.

Makes about 60 cookies.

Nutritional Information (per cookie): Calories: 125, Protein: 1 g, Carbohydrate: 19 g, Fiber: 1 g, Sugars: 13 g, Fat: 5 g, Saturated Fat: 2.5 g, Trans Fat: 0.1 g, Cholesterol: 15 mg, Sodium: 92 mg, Potassium: 15 mg

BAKING

ORANGE-GLAZED CRANBERRY RAISIN SQUARES

V

Best eaten with a fork, these squares are filled with cranberry sauce and golden raisins.

1¾ cups (425 mL) whole barley flour

½ cup (125 mL) all-purpose flour

¾ cup (175 mL) granulated sugar

¾ tsp (4 mL) baking powder

¾ tsp (4 mL) salt

¾ cup (175 mL) butter

2 eggs

½ cup (125 mL) milk

1 tsp (5 mL) almond extract

1 can (14 oz [398 mL]) whole berry cranberry sauce

½ cup (125 mL) golden raisins

1½ cups (375 mL) sifted icing sugar

3 Tbsp (45 mL) orange juice

1 Tbsp (15 mL) grated orange rind

Preheat oven to 400°F (200°C). Grease a 9 × 13 inch (23 × 33 cm) cake pan.

In a medium bowl, stir together barley flour, all-purpose flour, sugar, baking powder, and salt. Cut in butter until mixture is in pea-sized pieces. In another bowl, beat eggs, adding milk and almond extract. Add to flour mixture. Mix well. In a separate bowl, combine cranberry sauce and raisins. Spread half of the dough mixture in the pan, then spread cranberry mixture overtop. Drop 12 spoonfuls of remaining dough overtop of cranberries. Cranberry mixture will not be entirely covered. Bake for 25 to 30 minutes.

While squares are cooling, prepare glaze by mixing icing sugar, orange juice, and orange rind. Once squares are slightly cool, spread glaze overtop.

Makes 12 large or 24 small squares.

Nutritional Information (per large square): Calories: 373, Protein: 2 g, Carbohydrate: 62 g, Fiber: 3 g, Sugars: 42 g, Fat: 15 g, Saturated Fat: 8 g, Trans Fat: 0.5 g, Cholesterol: 63 mg, Sodium: 297 mg, Potassium: 95 mg

CHEWY CARAMEL SQUARES

These easy squares, mixed in one saucepan, make a mouthwatering treat.

¼ cup (60 mL) butter or margarine

1 cup (250 mL) lightly packed brown sugar

1 egg

1½ tsp (7 mL) vanilla

¾ cup (175 mL) whole barley flour

1 tsp (5 mL) baking powder

¼ tsp (1 mL) salt

¼ cup (60 mL) chopped nuts

¼ cup (60 mL) shredded coconut

Preheat oven to 350°F (180°C). Lightly grease an 8-inch (20 cm) square baking pan.

In a large saucepan over medium heat, melt butter or margarine. Remove from heat and stir in brown sugar, egg, and vanilla. Blend in flour, baking powder, salt, nuts, and coconut. Spread mixture into baking pan. Bake for 20 to 25 minutes or until set in center but still soft. Cool in pan on wire rack and cut into bars.

Makes about 24 bars.

Nutritional Information (per bar): Calories: 80, Protein: 1 g, Carbohydrate: 12 g, Fiber: 1 g, Sugars: 9 g, Fat: 4 g, Saturated Fat: 1.5 g, Trans Fat: 0.1 g, Cholesterol: 13 mg, Sodium: 65 mg, Potassium: 26 mg

DOUBLE CHOCOLATE BROWNIES

Ⓥ

These moist, fudgy brownies are made with barley flour and cocoa sweetened with honey. A topping of chocolate chips forms a delectable glaze.

¾ cup (175 mL) whole barley flour

½ cup (125 mL) unsweetened cocoa powder, sifted

¼ tsp (1 mL) salt

1 cup (250 mL) honey

½ cup (125 mL) butter or margarine, melted

2 eggs, lightly beaten

3 Tbsp (45 mL) water

1 tsp (5 mL) vanilla

½ cup (125 mL) chopped walnuts

⅓ cup (75 mL) semi-sweet chocolate chips

Preheat oven to 325°F (160°C). Grease the bottom of an 8-inch (20 cm) square baking pan.

In a large bowl, mix together flour, cocoa powder, and salt. Add honey, butter or margarine, eggs, water, and vanilla, then beat until smooth. Stir in nuts. Spread batter evenly in prepared pan. Sprinkle with chocolate chips. Bake for 30 to 40 minutes or until a cake tester or toothpick inserted in the center comes out clean. Let cool completely before cutting into brownies.

Makes approximately 20 brownies.

Nutritional Information (per brownie): Calories: 151, Protein: 2 g, Carbohydrate: 20 g, Fiber: 1 g, Sugars: 15 g, Fat: 9 g, Saturated Fat: 4 g, Trans Fat: 0.2 g, Cholesterol: 32 mg, Sodium: 77 mg, Potassium: 31 mg

CHOCOLATE-DIPPED ALMOND BISCOTTI

These almond biscotti are double baked and then dipped in chocolate, but the delicious results are well worth the extra steps.

1½ cups (375 mL) whole barley flour

1½ cups (375 mL) all-purpose flour

1½ tsp (7 mL) baking powder

¼ tsp (1 mL) salt

½ cup (125 mL) butter or margarine

¾ cup (175 mL) granulated sugar

2 eggs

1 tsp (5 mL) vanilla

½ tsp (2 mL) almond extract

½ cup (125 mL) blanched almonds, toasted and coarsely chopped

1 tsp (5 mL) grated orange rind

8 oz (225 g) (8 squares) semi-sweet or bittersweet chocolate

Preheat oven to 325°F (160°C). Lightly grease a cookie sheet.

In a small bowl, combine barley flour, all-purpose flour, baking powder, and salt. In a large mixing bowl, beat together butter and sugar until light and fluffy. Beat in eggs, one at a time. Stir in vanilla and almond extract, then almonds and orange rind. Stir in flour mixture just until blended.

On prepared cookie sheet, shape stiff dough into two 4-inch (10 cm) wide by ¾-inch (2 cm) thick loaves. Bake for 25 minutes. Cool loaves on wire rack for 5 minutes, then cut each loaf on the diagonal into ½-inch (1.5 cm) thick slices. Arrange slices cut side up on cookie sheets and bake until golden, about 10 minutes; turn over and bake other side until golden, about 10 minutes. Cool biscotti on rack.

Line a clean cookie sheet with parchment paper. Melt chocolate as directed on the package and dip one end of each biscotti into it, spreading with a spatula, if desired. Or drizzle chocolate over biscotti using a small spoon. Place on cookie sheet and refrigerate until chocolate sets, about 15 minutes.

Makes 24 biscotti.

Nutritional Information (per biscotti): Calories: 182, Protein: 3 g, Carbohydrate: 24 g, Fiber: 1 g, Sugars: 12 g, Fat: 10 g, Saturated Fat: 4.5 g, Trans Fat: 0.2 g, Cholesterol: 26 mg, Sodium: 87 mg, Potassium: 35 mg

SWEET TREATS

APPLE CRANBERRY CRISP

For extra flavor, use more than one kind of apple in this easy baked dessert. Serve warm or at room temperature, topped with whipped cream or ice cream.

½ cup (125 mL) granulated sugar

⅔ cup (150 mL) whole barley flour, divided

Grated rind of 1 lemon

4 large apples, peeled and sliced (4 cups [1 L])

2 cups (500 mL) fresh or frozen cranberries (see Barley Bit)

1¼ cups (310 mL) barley flakes

¾ cup (175 mL) packed brown sugar

1½ tsp (7 mL) ground cinnamon

¼ cup (60 mL) canola oil

Preheat oven to 375°F (190°C). Lightly grease a 9 × 13 inch (23 × 33 cm) baking dish.

In a large bowl, combine the granulated sugar, ⅓ cup (75 mL) of the barley flour, and the lemon rind. Mix in apples and cranberries. Spoon into baking dish. In a small bowl, combine barley flakes, remaining ⅓ cup (75 mL) of barley flour, brown sugar, and cinnamon. Toss with canola oil and spoon over fruit. Bake for 40 to 50 minutes or until apples are bubbling and topping is golden.

Makes 6 servings.

Nutritional Information (per serving, without whipped cream or ice cream): Calories: 408, Protein: 3 g, Carbohydrate: 82 g, Fiber: 8 g, Sugars: 54 g, Fat: 11 g, Saturated Fat: 0.5 g, Trans Fat: 0 g, Cholesterol: 0 mg, Sodium: 14 mg, Potassium: 159 mg

Barley Bit: Frozen cranberries can be used straight from the package.

RASPBERRY RHUBARB COBBLER

Ⓥ

Keep a stash of rhubarb in the freezer just so you can enjoy this warm, comforting dessert year-round. Serve with a puff of whipped cream.

3 cups (750 mL) sliced fresh (or frozen and thawed) rhubarb

1 cup (250 mL) granulated sugar, divided

2 Tbsp (30 mL) cornstarch

1 Tbsp (15 mL) water

1 cup (250 mL) fresh or frozen unsweetened raspberries (see Barley Bit)

1 cup (250 mL) whole barley flour

1½ tsp (7 mL) baking powder

¼ tsp (1 mL) salt

¼ cup (60 mL) butter

¼ cup (60 mL) milk

1 egg, slightly beaten

Preheat oven to 400°F (200°C).

In a saucepan, combine rhubarb, 1 cup (250 mL) less 2 tablespoons (30 mL) sugar, cornstarch, and water. Bring to a boil over medium heat, then cook while stirring for 1 minute. Stir in raspberries. Pour into a round 9-inch (23 cm) baking dish.

In a small bowl, combine barley flour, reserved 2 tablespoons (30 mL) sugar, baking powder, and salt. Cut in butter until mixture resembles coarse crumbs. In another small bowl, combine milk and egg, then add to flour mixture, stirring just until dry ingredients are moistened. Spoon over hot rhubarb mixture. Bake 20 to 25 minutes. Serve warm.

Makes 6 servings.

Nutritional Information (per serving): Calories: 311, Protein: 2 g, Carbohydrate: 55 g, Fiber: 5 g, Sugars: 36 g, Fat: 12 g, Saturated Fat: 5 g, Trans Fat: 0.3 g, Cholesterol: 53 mg, Sodium: 275 mg, Potassium: 235 mg

Barley Bit: If using frozen raspberries, do not thaw.

BERRY BARLEY SHORTCAKE

A simple-to-make shortcake is often served at Pat's house. This version with rustic cakes made from barley flour is one of the best when topped with mixed berries and whipped cream.

1 cup (250 mL) whole barley flour

1 cup (250 mL) all-purpose flour

⅓ cup (75 mL) granulated sugar

1 Tbsp (15 mL) baking powder

1 tsp (5 mL) grated lemon rind

½ tsp (2 mL) salt

½ cup (125 mL) butter or margarine

1 egg, beaten

½ cup (125 mL) milk (approximately)

1 cup (250 mL) whipping cream

1 Tbsp (15 mL) icing sugar

6 cups (1.5 L) mixed fresh berries (sliced strawberries, raspberries, Saskatoons, or blueberries)

Preheat oven to 450°F (230°C). Grease a baking sheet.

In a medium bowl, combine barley flour, all-purpose flour, sugar, baking powder, lemon rind, and salt. Cut in butter until mixture resembles coarse crumbs. Add egg and enough milk to moisten dry ingredients. Shape dough into 6 mounds on the baking sheet. Bake for 12 to 15 minutes or until golden brown. Cool.

Whip cream, adding icing sugar. When cool, split cakes in half horizontally; spread each bottom half with whipped cream and a sprinkle of berries. Cover with top halves, more whipped cream, and remaining berries.

Makes 6 servings.

Nutritional Information (per serving): Calories: 560, Protein: 8 g, Carbohydrate: 63 g, Fiber: 9 g, Sugars: 23 g, Fat: 32 g, Saturated Fat: 19 g, Trans Fat: 1 g, Cholesterol: 129 mg, Sodium: 553 mg, Potassium: 283 mg

PRAIRIE STREUSEL-TOPPED CAKE

In mid-summer, you'd expect to find this cake in a farm kitchen, or perhaps your neighbor would bring one when she came to visit. Serve as a snack or warm with ice cream for dessert.

Cake

¾ cup (175 mL) whole barley flour

¾ cup (175 mL) all-purpose flour

4½ tsp (22 mL) baking powder

¼ tsp (1 mL) salt

⅓ cup (75 mL) butter or margarine

¾ cup (175 mL) granulated sugar

2 eggs

¾ cup (175 mL) milk

4 cups (1 L) Saskatoon berries

1 cup (250 mL) sliced fresh (or frozen and thawed) rhubarb

Topping

¾ cup (175 mL) whole barley flour

¾ cup (175 mL) all-purpose flour

½ cup (125 mL) granulated sugar

⅓ cup (75 mL) butter or margarine

1½ tsp (7 mL) ground cinnamon

Preheat oven to 350°F (180°C). Grease a 9 × 13 inch (23 × 33 cm) baking dish.

In a small bowl, combine the barley flour, all-purpose flour, baking powder, and salt. In a large bowl, cream butter or margarine and sugar. Beat in eggs and milk. Gradually stir in dry ingredients. When mixed, pour batter into the baking dish. Sprinkle Saskatoon berries and rhubarb overtop of batter.

To make topping, combine the barley flour, all-purpose flour, sugar, butter or margarine, and cinnamon in a small bowl, using a pastry blender or fingertips. Sprinkle evenly overtop of the cake batter. Bake for 40 to 45 minutes.

Makes 10 servings.

Nutritional Information (per serving): Calories: 392, Protein: 5 g, Carbohydrate: 61 g, Fiber: 5 g, Sugars: 27 g, Fat: 16 g, Saturated Fat: 8 g, Trans Fat: 0.5 g, Cholesterol: 72 mg, Sodium: 353 mg, Potassium: 166 mg

PEACH UPSIDE-DOWN GINGER CAKE

Here's a delicious way to use fresh peaches. But frozen ones that have been thawed will do, too. Once baked, the cake is turned upside down, leaving the peaches on top. Yummy as is or topped with whipped cream!

2½ cups (625 mL) sliced fresh peaches

1 cup (250 mL) granulated sugar, divided

2 tsp (10 mL) ground cinnamon, divided

1 tsp (5 mL) grated orange rind

1 cup (250 mL) whole barley flour

1 cup (250 mL) all-purpose flour

2 tsp (10 mL) baking powder

1 tsp (5 mL) ground ginger

½ tsp (2 mL) salt

¼ tsp (1 mL) baking soda

⅓ cup (75 mL) butter or margarine, softened

1 egg

¾ cup (175 mL) molasses

¾ cup (175 mL) buttermilk

Preheat oven to 350°F (180°C). Line a 9-inch (23 cm) square pan with parchment paper and lightly grease.

In a medium bowl, mix peaches with ½ cup (125 mL) of the sugar, 1 teaspoon (5 mL) of the cinnamon, and the orange rind. Arrange overlapping peach slices in a circle in the bottom of the pan. In a medium bowl, combine the barley flour, all-purpose flour, baking powder, ginger, salt, baking soda, and remaining 1 teaspoon (5 mL) of cinnamon. In a large bowl, cream butter or margarine with remaining ½ cup (125 mL) of sugar. Add egg and whip until fluffy, then mix in molasses. Add flour mixture to butter mixture, alternating with buttermilk and starting and ending with flour mixture. Stir after each addition until just mixed. Pour batter over peaches. Bake for 45 to 50 minutes or until cake springs back when lightly touched. Let cake cool on rack for 10 minutes, then run a knife around the sides of the pan and invert onto a serving dish.

Makes approximately 16 pieces.

Nutritional Information (per piece): Calories: 199, Protein: 2 g, Carbohydrate: 38 g, Fiber: 2 g, Sugars: 24 g, Fat: 6 g, Saturated Fat: 2.5 g, Trans Fat: 0.2 g, Cholesterol: 23 mg, Sodium: 194 mg, Potassium: 298 mg

CHOCOLATE CAKE

(V)

This delicious chocolate cake is a testament to the versatility of barley flour.

2 cups (500 mL) granulated sugar

2 eggs

2 tsp (10 mL) vanilla

⅔ cup (150 mL) canola oil

3 cups (750 mL) whole barley flour

⅔ cup (150 mL) cocoa powder

2 tsp (10 mL) baking powder

2 tsp (10 mL) baking soda

1 tsp (5 mL) salt

2 cups (500 mL) boiling water

Preheat oven to 350°F (180°C). Grease a 9 × 13 inch (23 × 33 cm) pan or a 12-cup Bundt pan.

In a large bowl, beat sugar, eggs, vanilla, and oil for 4 minutes. In another bowl, sift together barley flour, cocoa powder, baking powder, baking soda, and salt. Starting and ending with dry ingredients, stir dry ingredients into liquid mixture, alternating with boiling water. Beat until smooth. Pour batter into the pan. Bake for 45 minutes or until center springs back when lightly touched. Cool, then, if desired, dust with icing sugar or frost with your favorite icing.

Makes approximately 24 servings.

Nutritional Information (per serving): Calories: 181, Protein: 1 g, Carbohydrate: 28 g, Fiber: 2 g, Sugars: 17 g, Fat: 9 g, Saturated Fat: 0.5 g, Trans Fat: 0 g, Cholesterol: 16 mg, Sodium: 240 mg, Potassium: 6 mg

ZUCCHINI LEMON CAKE

Here's a tasty way to use up plentiful zucchini. Plus, the cake will keep a lot longer in the freezer than the vegetable will in your crisper. The lemon sugar glaze is optional but does add a delicious touch of sweetness to the cake.

Cake

3 eggs

1⅓ cups (325 mL) granulated sugar

¾ cup (175 mL) canola oil

¼ cup (60 mL) lemon juice

2 cups (500 mL) grated unpeeled zucchini

2 cups (500 mL) whole barley flour

1 tsp (5 mL) baking soda

1 tsp (5 mL) baking powder

½ tsp (2 mL) salt

1 cup (250 mL) chopped walnuts

Glaze (optional)

3 Tbsp (45 mL) lemon juice

2 cups (500 mL) icing sugar

Preheat oven to 350°F (180°C). Grease well a 9 × 13 inch (23 × 33 cm) baking pan.

In a large bowl, beat eggs, sugar, oil, and lemon juice. Fold in grated zucchini. In another bowl, sift together flour, baking soda, baking powder, and salt. Add walnuts. Gently fold into zucchini mixture. Pour into pan. Bake for 40 to 50 minutes, until a toothpick inserted comes out clean. Let cool.

If using the lemon glaze: in a medium bowl, stir lemon juice into icing sugar. For a thinner glaze, add more juice; for a thicker glaze, you may need to add more sugar. When desired thickness is achieved, pour glaze over cake.

Makes 12 servings.

Nutritional Information (per serving, with glaze): Calories: 436, Protein: 3 g, Carbohydrate: 59 g, Fiber: 3 g, Sugars: 43 g, Fat: 25 g, Saturated Fat: 2 g, Trans Fat: 0 g, Cholesterol: 48 mg, Sodium: 253 mg, Potassium: 145 mg

ORANGE SPICE CUPCAKES

The nutty flavor of barley flour combines with orange rind and spices in this easy-to-make basic cupcake recipe. Frost with a store-bought frosting or your favorite homemade vanilla or cream cheese frosting.

2 cups (500 mL) whole barley flour

1 Tbsp (15 mL) baking powder

1 Tbsp (15 mL) grated orange rind

1 tsp (5 mL) ground cinnamon

½ tsp (2 mL) ground allspice

½ tsp (2 mL) ground nutmeg

½ tsp (2 mL) salt

⅓ cup (75 mL) butter or margarine, softened

1 cup (250 mL) granulated sugar

1 egg

¾ cup (175 mL) milk

Preheat oven to 375°F (190°C). Line medium muffin pans with paper liners, or lightly grease.

In a medium bowl, combine barley flour, baking powder, orange rind, cinnamon, allspice, nutmeg, and salt. In a large bowl, cream butter or margarine. Beat in sugar, then beat in egg. Stir in flour mixture in thirds, alternating with milk. Spoon batter into muffin pans, filling cups slightly more than half full. Bake for 20 to 25 minutes or until a cake tester or toothpick inserted in center comes out clean. Cool in pans on wire racks for 5 minutes, then remove cupcakes from pans. If desired, when cool, frost each cupcake with 2 tablespoons (30 mL) of your favorite cream cheese icing.

Makes 16 medium cupcakes.

Nutritional Information (per cupcake, without icing): Calories: 289, Protein: 2 g, Carbohydrate: 48 g, Fiber: 3 g, Sugars: 35 g, Fat: 10 g, Saturated Fat: 4 g, Trans Fat: 1.5 g, Cholesterol: 23 mg, Sodium: 257 mg, Potassium: 25 mg

STEAMED CARROT PUDDING WITH CARAMEL SAUCE

This yummy cool-weather dessert freezes beautifully. Serve with the caramel sauce, or use a rum or lemon sauce.

Pudding

1½ cups (375 mL) whole barley flour

1½ tsp (7 mL) baking soda

1 tsp (5 mL) ground cinnamon

½ tsp (2 mL) ground nutmeg

¼ tsp (1 mL) ground cloves

1½ cups (375 mL) raisins

3 eggs

1½ cups (375 mL) granulated sugar

2 large carrots, finely shredded (1½ cups [375 mL])

2 medium to large potatoes, finely shredded (1½ cups [375 mL])

Caramel Sauce

1½ cups (375 mL) packed dark brown sugar

2 cups (500 mL) boiling water

3 Tbsp (45 mL) cornstarch

¼ tsp (1 mL) salt

2 Tbsp (30 mL) cold water

3 Tbsp (45 mL) butter or margarine

1 tsp (5 mL) vanilla extract

½ tsp (2 mL) ground nutmeg

In a large bowl, stir together barley flour, baking soda, cinnamon, nutmeg, and cloves. Stir in raisins. In a food processor or blender, place eggs, sugar, carrots, and potatoes. Process until mixture is smooth, then stir into dry ingredients.

Grease a 2-quart (2 L) heat-resistant glass or ceramic bowl. Pour batter into the bowl; cover with foil and secure foil with a string. Place bowl in a Dutch oven or deep pot. Pour enough boiling water into the Dutch oven to come 1 inch (2.5 cm) up the sides of the bowl.

Place the lid on Dutch oven and allow to steam for 1½ to 2 hours or until a cake tester or toothpick inserted in the center comes out clean. Invert pudding onto a serving plate.

Meanwhile, prepare the caramel sauce. In a large saucepan with a heavy bottom over medium heat, melt brown sugar. Stir occasionally and let brown slightly. Remove from heat and stir in measured boiling water. Return to heat and cook until smooth. In a small bowl, mix cornstarch, salt, and cold water; gradually add to the sugar mixture, stirring to prevent lumping. Simmer over low heat for 5 to 10 minutes or until thickened and clear. Remove from heat and stir in butter or margarine, vanilla, and nutmeg.

Serve pudding while still warm. Pour a little caramel sauce over each serving and top with a dollop of vanilla ice cream or whipped cream, if desired.

Makes 8 servings.

Nutritional Information (per serving, with sauce): Calories: 591, Protein: 5 g, Carbohydrate: 130 g, Fiber: 6 g, Sugars: 102 g, Fat: 10 g, Saturated Fat: 3.5 g, Trans Fat: 0.1 g, Cholesterol: 84 mg, Sodium: 407 mg, Potassium: 374 mg

OLD-FASHIONED BAKED BARLEY PUDDING

When you crave an old-fashioned sweet treat, try this modern version of a creamy baked pudding. Dried cranberries can be substituted for raisins. This pudding can also be served for breakfast or brunch.

2¾ cups (675 mL) water

⅔ cup (150 mL) pearl or pot barley

1 tsp (5 mL) salt

2 eggs

1⅓ cups (325 mL) milk

¼ cup (60 mL) packed brown sugar

1 Tbsp (15 mL) butter or margarine, melted

1 tsp (5 mL) vanilla

⅓ cup (75 mL) raisins

½ tsp (2 mL) grated lemon rind

1 tsp (5 mL) lemon juice

In a medium saucepan, bring measured water to a boil; add barley and salt. Reduce heat, cover pan, and simmer for 45 minutes or until barley is tender. Allow to cool.

Preheat oven to 325°F (160°C). Grease well a 1½-quart (1.5 L) baking dish.

In a medium bowl, combine eggs, milk, brown sugar, butter or margarine, and vanilla; beat well. Add cooked barley, raisins, lemon rind, and lemon juice. Turn into prepared baking dish. Set dish into a larger baking pan and place in oven. Pour hot water into the larger pan to within 1 inch (2.5 cm) of the top of the pudding. Bake uncovered for 1 hour or until a knife inserted in the center comes out clean. Serve hot or cold, garnished, if desired, with fresh berries and a sprig of mint.

Makes 6 servings.

Nutritional Information (per serving): Calories: 209, Protein: 6 g, Carbohydrate: 36 g, Fiber: 4 g, Sugars: 18 g, Fat: 4.5 g, Saturated Fat: 2 g, Trans Fat: 0.1 g, Cholesterol: 72 mg, Sodium: 466 mg, Potassium: 248 mg

EASY BARLEY PIE CRUST

Barley flour adds old-fashioned goodness to this pie crust, which is made in a food processor. Omit the sugar when the crust is to be used for savory pies, such as quiche.

¾ cup (175 mL) whole barley flour

½ cup (125 mL) all-purpose flour

2 Tbsp (30 mL) granulated sugar (optional)

¼ cup (60 mL) cold butter

4–5 Tbsp (60–75 mL) cold water

In food processor, combine barley flour, all-purpose flour, sugar (if using), and butter. Process just until mixture resembles coarse crumbs. Add water and process just until mixture holds together. Shape into a ball. Roll out according to specific pie recipe instructions.

Makes enough dough for one 9-inch (23 cm) single pie crust.

Nutritional Information (per pie crust): Calories: 915, Protein: 7 g, Carbohydrate: 107 g, Fiber: 12 g, Sugars: 2 g, Fat: 59 g, Saturated Fat: 29 g, Trans Fat: 2 g, Cholesterol: 122 mg, Sodium: 409 mg, Potassium: 81 mg

RUSTIC APPLE PIE

This easy-to-make old-fashioned pie is always a hit with the family. Warm before serving. It's delicious unadorned or served with a small wedge of cheddar cheese or a spoonful of whipped cream or ice cream.

Easy Barley Pie Crust (p. 222)

6–8 large apples (about 8 cups [2 L])

½ cup (125 mL) granulated sugar

2 Tbsp (30 mL) whole barley flour

1 tsp (5 mL) ground cinnamon

1 Tbsp (15 mL) milk

1 Tbsp (15 mL) coarse sugar

Preheat oven to 475°F (240°C).

On a lightly floured surface, roll pie pastry into a thin circle, 14 to 16 inches (36–40 cm) wide. Fold in half and gently lift into a 9-inch (23 cm) pie plate. Unfold pastry and, using fingers, press against the bottom edges of pie plate. Let excess pastry hang over the side of the pie plate.

Peel, core, and thinly slice apples. Turn into a medium bowl. In a small bowl, combine sugar, barley flour, and cinnamon. Sprinkle over apples, tossing to mix well. Turn apples into pie shell; gently press down and smooth top. Fold pastry over apples, overlapping where necessary. Pastry may not cover center and edges will be ragged. Brush top of pastry with milk and then sprinkle with coarse sugar. Place pie in oven for 15 minutes. Reduce temperature to 375°F (190°C) and bake until apples are tender and pastry is golden, about 35 minutes. Let cool on a wire rack.

Makes one 9-inch (23 cm) pie (8 servings).

Nutritional Information (per serving, ⅛ of pie): Calories: 233, Protein: 1 g, Carbohydrate: 44 g, Fiber: 4 g, Sugars: 26 g, Fat: 8 g, Saturated Fat: 3.5 g, Trans Fat: 0.2 g, Cholesterol: 15 mg, Sodium: 53 mg, Potassium: 131 mg

PUMPKIN PIE

Serve this golden pumpkin pie topped with whipped cream or a combination of Greek yogurt and whipped cream flavored with a dash of brown sugar and vanilla. Dust with ground cinnamon.

Easy Barley Pie Crust (p. 222)

1 can (14 oz [398 mL]) pumpkin purée

1 cup (250 mL) packed dark brown sugar

1¼ cups (310 mL) 2% evaporated milk

2 eggs

½ tsp (2 mL) ground cinnamon

¼ tsp (1 mL) ground ginger

¼ tsp (1 mL) salt

Pinch ground nutmeg

Pinch ground cloves

Preheat oven to 425°F (220°C).

On a lightly floured surface, roll pie crust dough into a circle slightly larger than a 9-inch (23 cm) pie plate. Gently fold in half and lift into pie plate. Pinch over-hanging pastry to form an edge. Refrigerate for 15 minutes.

In a large bowl, whisk pumpkin purée, brown sugar, evaporated milk, eggs, cinnamon, ginger, salt, nutmeg, and cloves. Pour into prepared pie crust. Bake for 15 minutes. Reduce heat to 350°F (180°C) and continue baking for 45 minutes or until a knife or toothpick inserted in the center comes out clean. Place on a wire rack to cool.

Makes one 9-inch (23 cm) pie (8 servings).

Nutritional Information (per serving, ⅛ of pie): Calories: 287, Protein: 6 g, Carbohydrate: 48 g, Fiber: 4 g, Sugars: 32 g, Fat: 10 g, Saturated Fat: 4 g, Trans Fat: 0.2 g, Cholesterol: 70 mg, Sodium: 195 mg, Potassium: 189 mg

PINEAPPLE BARLEY MOUSSE

To end a special dinner, serve this creamy barley pineapple mousse topped with colorful fresh fruit.

2 cups (500 mL) pot or pearl barley

7 cups (1.75 L) water

1 package (3.6 oz [102 g]) instant vanilla pudding mix

2 cups (500 mL) milk

1 package (8 oz [250 g]) cream cheese, softened

1 can (14 oz [398 mL]) crushed pineapple

1½ cups (375 mL) whipping cream

2 Tbsp (30 mL) icing sugar

¼ tsp (1 mL) vanilla or rum extract

Banana, kiwi, mandarin orange segments, raspberries, for garnish

In a large saucepan, combine barley and water. Bring to a boil, then reduce heat to simmer. Cover pan and cook for 40 minutes. Drain and chill. In a medium bowl, prepare pudding mix with milk, following package directions. In a large bowl, beat softened cream cheese until smooth. Fold in pudding mix, crushed pineapple, including juice, and cooked barley. In another bowl, whip cream, adding icing sugar and vanilla or rum extract; fold into cream cheese mixture. Refrigerate until ready to spoon into serving dishes. Garnish with fruit and serve.

Makes 12 servings.

Nutritional Information (per serving, excludes fresh fruit): Calories: 367, Protein: 7 g, Carbohydrate: 44 g, Fiber: 6 g, Sugars: 16 g, Fat: 19 g, Saturated Fat: 11 g, Trans Fat: 0.5 g, Cholesterol: 66 mg, Sodium: 155 mg, Potassium: 250 mg

BARLEY WATER

This refreshing drink can be served chilled or hot. The cooked barley can be refrigerated or frozen to add to salads, soups, or casseroles.

8 cups (2 L) water

½ cup (125 mL) pot or pearl barley

2 Tbsp (30 mL) granulated sugar, or to taste

Pinch of salt

Rind of 1 small lemon

¼ cup (60 mL) lemon juice

In a large saucepan over high heat, bring water to a boil. Add barley and bring water back to a boil. Reduce heat, cover pan, and simmer gently for 2 hours. Strain liquid from barley into a container, reserving barley for later use. Allow liquid to cool slightly, then add sugar, salt, lemon rind, and lemon juice. Serve chilled or as a hot drink.

Makes about 6 cups.

Nutritional Information (per cup): Calories: 19, Protein: 0 g, Carbohydrate: 5 g, Fiber: 0 g, Sugars: 4 g, Fat: 0 g, Saturated Fat: 0 g, Trans Fat: 0 g, Cholesterol: 0 mg, Sodium: 34 mg, Potassium: 15 mg

INDEX

ACKNOWLEDGMENTS

We would like to thank all the people and organizations who worked with us to bring this book to fruition. First and foremost, we'd like to thank Alberta Barley farmers and their families who believe in eating well and enjoying the products they grow. We'd also like to thank Lisa Skierka for her foresight in getting a book about barley on the shelves.

Countless others assisted in making this book possible: Sue Spicer, our talented food stylist; Wendi Hiebert for our nutrient analysis; Bryce Meyer for embracing the new world of food photography; Michael Interisano for his gorgeous photos of barley fields; and Anne-Marie Bruzga-Luchak for support throughout the process. Special thanks to Karen Hoover for her excellent assistance in getting our first large go-round of photography organized; Jane Dummer, who we called upon whenever we needed extra advice on nutrition; and Linda Malcolmson, and the Canadian International Grains Institute, who has done so much in the pursuit of barley food products.

Key to getting this off the ground was the work of Dr. Nancy Ames and her team from Agriculture and Agri-Food Canada, who worked tirelessly to research and present the scientific information for the barley health claim.

Additional thanks go out to the Alberta Barley communications team for their ongoing support, especially Tyler Difley, whose editing skills were greatly appreciated.

Thank you to TouchWood Editions and our publisher, Ruth Linka, who made our vision a reality and provided guidance as the manuscript came together. Special thanks to our editor Cailey Cavallin, designer Pete Kohut, and publicist Emily Shorthouse for making this a truly exceptional book.

And last but best, our families, friends, and colleagues, who have provided inspiration, ideas, and cooking equipment, as well as serving as tasters throughout our careers. We hope we haven't missed anyone, because this list could go on and on.

Enjoy *Go Barley: Modern Recipes for an Ancient Grain*—and continue to watch the GoBarley.com website for more recipes and great food information.

PAT INGLIS is a professional home economist and food writer who throughout her career has worked with American and Canadian food producers and manufacturers, creating tasty, nutritious recipes that showcase their products.

Initially, she worked for a major food manufacturer, Nabisco, as supervisor of consumer publicity. After marrying a Montrealer, she became food writer for the *Montreal Gazette.* In 1981 she moved to Alberta with a growing family. There she continued as a consultant for many Alberta food producers.

Pat also served as a food safety information officer for a nationwide food safety hotline, a position that put her in touch with consumers and media on food safety issues all over Canada. She wrote and directed the production of educational fact sheets, news releases, radio and TV scripts, and educational presentations, and she also prepared website content.

Recently, a friendship with co-author Linda Whitworth got her started developing a "few recipes" that featured barley grains and flour. One good recipe led to another and soon, as her family and friends will attest, she was immersed in creating a wide variety of recipes for these versatile products.

Pat Inglis has a bachelor of science in food and nutrition from Douglas College, Rutgers University in New Jersey. She has completed upgrading courses in food safety and food microbiology offered by the University of Alberta.

LINDA WHITWORTH is becoming known as the "queen of barley" in her work promoting barley as a healthy grain in Canada, the United States and abroad.

In her day job, Linda is the market development manager for Alberta Barley, as well as a home economist with an extensive background in the food industry. She is the host of "Linda in the Kitchen" on gobarley.com, which profiles recipes from this cookbook and other sources.

In the past, Linda worked in retail management, mall management, and marketing. She was also a home economist for Calgary Co-op, where she worked on the marketing team to decide on listings for grocery stores, acted as a Co-op consumer liaison, and promoted Co-op products.

Linda has an extensive background with agriculture organizations, working as a consultant for 15 years between the Alberta Cattle Commission, Alberta Egg Producers, Beef Information Centre, Nova Scotia Egg Producers, and Alberta Beef.

In the spring of 2013, Linda completed a successful media tour promoting barley across Canada and informing consumers about the health benefits of eating barley.

Linda holds a bachelor of science in home economics from the University of Alberta and has taken additional courses in building management, marketing, and small business development. She was born in Regina, Saskatchewan, but moved to Calgary, Alberta, when she was four years old. She also lived in Nova Scotia for eight and a half years, before returning to Calgary, where she currently resides.